*My Mother*
*My Daughter*
*My Sister*
*My Self*

*MY MOTHER*
*Faith Collins*

**MY DAUGHTER**
Laura McCarty

MY SISTER
Penny Bagby

**MY SELF**
Patricia Ruth

**Three Generations of Poetry**

JPAR Publishing
Austin
2014

United States Copyright Office
Preregistration Number: PRE000007524
Effective Date of Preregistration: 10/15/2014
Class(es) of Work: Literary Work in Book Form

Title: My Mother, My Daughter, My Sister, My Self
Three Generations of Poetry


JPAR Publishing, Austin
Editor: Penny Ingle Bagby
Cover Design: Laura McCarty

ISBN#   978-0-692-31250-6
E-book# 978-0-692-31287-2

Library of Congress 2014

## Dedication

To George J. Williams, Sr., long dead muse, who gave us joy, inspiration, and bequeathed genes so that we, like him, would ache and sing.

**Daughters of the family of George**

## Contents

MY MOTHER ................................................................. 1

The Primitive ................................................................ 3

Who Art In Heaven ..................................................... 4

Merry-Go-Round ......................................................... 5

With Strings Tied ......................................................... 6

Confessional ................................................................. 7

Odyssey ......................................................................... 8

The Enlightened ........................................................... 9

Backward Slider ......................................................... 10

Legacy .......................................................................... 11

Selection ...................................................................... 12

Anacahuita .................................................................. 13

Serpentes Doggeralis ................................................. 14

On Weeping ................................................................ 16

Prayer .......................................................................... 17

Spring Organum ........................................................ 18

Moonflood .................................................................. 19

Long Distance Camera .............................................. 20

Pavane ......................................................................... 21

Death in Mexico ........................................................ 22

| | |
|---|---|
| Respite | 23 |
| Inland Alien | 24 |
| Mea Culpa | 25 |
| Illusion | 26 |
| Lucifer or Lochinvar! | 27 |
| East Texas Morning | 28 |
| Ah, Eve | 29 |
| Hosea's Wife | 30 |
| Ezekiel | 31 |
| Sic Transit | 32 |
| Nolle Prosequi | 33 |
| 40 Knots | 34 |
| Eden's Exile | 35 |
| Lot's Wife | 36 |
| Flight To Zion | 37 |
| The Box | 38 |
| VOWS | 39 |
| Accounting | 40 |
| Impotence | 41 |
| For Crying Out Loud | 42 |
| Façade | 43 |

| | |
|---|---|
| Dialogue | 44 |
| Summation | 45 |
| Stones from the Jordan | 46 |
| Impasse | 47 |
| Passage | 48 |
| Lonely Places | 49 |
| Discards | 50 |
| The Unburdened | 51 |
| Reckoning | 52 |
| Nightfall | 53 |
| Disconnect | 54 |
| At A Grave | 55 |
| The Delivery | 56 |
| Roses | 57 |
| Durable Foe | 58 |
| The Challenge | 59 |
| Of Saints and Sinners, Mostly Sinners | 60 |
| The Tally | 61 |
| The Valley Boy's Homecoming | 62 |
| After The Blake Exam | 63 |
| Le Professeur | 64 |

| | |
|---|---|
| Number Twenty-One | 65 |
| The Happy Boys | 66 |
| Barren | 67 |
| Silent Witnesses | 68 |
| Deprivation | 70 |
| Solitary Night-Shift Man | 70 |
| The Slow One | 72 |
| riddle | 73 |
| Confrontation | 74 |
| Loren Eiseley | 75 |
| Et je rapelle | 76 |
| Rain | 77 |
| Spring Rain | 78 |
| July in Houston | 79 |
| Mowing In Summer | 80 |
| June of '67 | 81 |
| Mirror | 82 |
| Child of Mine | 83 |
| Victory Sonnet | 84 |
| On Making Poetry | 85 |
| Bio: Faith Patricia Williams Ingle Collins | 86 |

MY DAUGHTER .................................................................... 89

Map of the World............................................................... 91

The Caretaker ..................................................................... 92

I dislocated my heart to silence the belly of my soul............... 94

Turning the Dirt ................................................................... 96

The Placid Warrior .............................................................. 98

Journey ................................................................................ 99

Observatory Place.............................................................. 100

The Weight of You.............................................................102

To Maya...............................................................................104

Story on the Rim ............................................................... 105

Saturday Chores................................................................. 106

Painted Woman/Painted Fathers...................................... 107

Brief Sensations ................................................................. 108

Listening to Kuwait ........................................................... 109

Texas Tunes ....................................................................... 110

Meet Me Beneath the Sitka Spruce .................................. 111

Reoccurring........................................................................ 112

Peach Colored Pills............................................................ 113

The Fig Thief...................................................................... 114

New Orleans Goodbye...................................................... 116

Fly By Love ........................................................................... 117
Radiology .............................................................................. 118
Morning Surprise ................................................................. 121
Sometimes ............................................................................. 122
Blessed Curse ....................................................................... 124
Viens à moi ........................................................................... 125
I don't think swings were made for women's hips ............... 126
Before the morning rises ..................................................... 127
The Benediction ................................................................... 128
When August turns to October .......................................... 130
Bio: Laura P. McCarty ......................................................... 131
MY SISTER ........................................................................... 133
Wordsworth — USA, 1992 .................................................. 135
Sentimental Journey ............................................................ 136
Re-vision ............................................................................... 137
Death Was Different Then .................................................. 138
Piece of Glass ....................................................................... 140
The Question — A Villanelle ............................................. 142
The Friend ............................................................................. 143
Jackrabbits ............................................................................ 144
Feather in the Wind ............................................................. 145

| | |
|---|---|
| Insolent Insomnia | 146 |
| Cottontails | 148 |
| Shhh … | 149 |
| May-lstrom | 150 |
| Persistence | 151 |
| Margarita with Salt | 152 |
| The Drought | 153 |
| Escape Plan | 154 |
| F o g | 155 |
| Second Verse | 156 |
| The Butter Knows | 157 |
| Recess in Tynan | 158 |
| Endowment | 159 |
| A Tie That Binds | 160 |
| Facsimile | 162 |
| Chalk Story | 163 |
| Dispossessed | 164 |
| Image | 165 |
| To My Mother (Mother's Day, 1979) | 166 |
| Forgiving Child | 167 |
| Petition — A Villanelle | 168 |
| Ah, Tchaikovsky! | 169 |

| | |
|---|---:|
| White Beauty | 170 |
| Conflict! | 171 |
| A Soldier's Peace | 172 |
| The Praying of the Creed | 173 |
| New Beginnings — A Villanelle | 178 |
| Personalities in Wood | 179 |
| Kaleidoscope | 180 |
| Palette | 181 |
| Mood Music | 182 |
| Esperanza | 183 |
| The Wedding Jewels | 184 |
| Residue | 185 |
| Exposed | 186 |
| Oaken | 187 |
| Transplanted | 188 |
| Requiem for Discovery | 189 |
| Spring Cleaning | 190 |
| Interview with Discovery | 192 |
| Vernal Exhibitionists | 194 |
| Vanity of Vanities | 195 |
| LunarRitual | 196 |
| The Doves | 198 |
| Lament | 199 |

| | |
|---|---|
| Sweeping Up Shards | 200 |
| Family Anthology | 201 |
| Brief Sojourn | 202 |
| Writing Poetry | 203 |
| Creating | 204 |
| Bio: Penny Faith Ingle Bagby | 205 |
| MY SELF | 207 |
| Forest Oasis | 209 |
| Song of a Kentucky Visit | 210 |
| The Day in the Navy Dress | 212 |
| Mirage | 214 |
| Far Sojourner | 215 |
| Turning Aside | 216 |
| Lament from a Fig Tree | 217 |
| Cleo's Snake | 218 |
| Showtime | 220 |
| Moving On | 221 |
| Porter For My Dreams | 222 |
| Drought | 224 |

| | |
|---|---|
| Grabbing the Ring | 225 |
| Life's Bookkeeping | 226 |
| Prayer at Seventeen | 227 |
| Daughter Mine | 228 |
| Unarmed | 229 |
| And What Did You Do with the Gown? | 230 |
| Long Gone Memories | 231 |
| Delaware Road | 232 |
| Midnight Tune | 233 |
| Passing By | 234 |
| The Face in the Jar | 235 |
| Kite Strings | 236 |
| Long Distance | 237 |
| Dream Raker | 238 |
| Separation | 239 |
| Insight | 240 |
| The Visit | 241 |
| Eclipse | 242 |
| Cry for Vietnam | 243 |
| Peaches | 244 |
| Heartwaves | 245 |

Dream Capsules .................................................................. 246

Lucy Lee ............................................................................. 247

Displaced ........................................................................... 248

Nightmares ........................................................................ 249

Clock Clicks ....................................................................... 250

People ................................................................................. 252

Solo ..................................................................................... 253

Chance Encounter ............................................................. 254

Night Call .......................................................................... 255

New Year's Day ................................................................ 256

The Vigil ............................................................................ 258

Void .................................................................................... 260

Breaking the Tape in the Nuclear Arms Race ............... 261

Album ................................................................................. 262

Conflagration .................................................................... 263

Retrospect .......................................................................... 264

Reprise ............................................................................... 265

Belief .................................................................................. 266

Care Packages ................................................................... 267

Comet ................................................................................. 268

Enigma ............................................................................... 269

The Bus Ticket .................................................................. 270

The Review ........................................................................ 272

| | |
|---|---|
| Holy Weak | 274 |
| Taking Out the Seam | 275 |
| Morning | 276 |
| Ice Palaces | 277 |
| Place of Rest | 278 |
| Ennui | 279 |
| Bargain | 280 |
| After The End | 281 |
| Prospecting | 282 |
| Bio: Patricia Ingle McCarty Castrinos Ruth | 283 |
| INDEX | 285 |

# *MY MOTHER*

## *Alien Soul*

## *Faith Collins*

## The Primitive

I have a timid soul
But my dreams are wild,
Roaming a brooding forest
The shadow of a raptor's wing
Rips the cold air
Above a scuttling rodent,
To leave blood upon the snow.

I have a timid soul
But my dream is wild,
Like a scarred and solitary giant,
Riveted by lightning,
Stands yet in productive death
While creatures soft and small
Claim squatter's rights
And build a nest.

I am a timid soul, but
I dream it wild
To follow the predatory wash
Diminishing the long edges
Of soft sands,
Hearing 'hush hush'
As the waves break
Over slow, emerging crabs
While the turtles bring forth
Their tough-skinned eggs
To secrete them in a dig
With only the moon a silent witness,
Surveying with ancient eye
The fecund sea.

**Who Art In Heaven**

God pity the poor Adam
Who tempted fate,
Turning from insular one-ness
To take a mate.

God pity the poor fool
Who, ravished, found
That weapons suited to hand
Could conquer ground.

God pity the poor stumbler,
Waking man,
Gone forth to meet his mind—
Uncharted land.

God grant to each lone exile
Wandering still,
Someday to regain Eden
Within Thy will.

## Merry-Go-Round

The merry-go-round
Has a beckoning sound
For the heart's holiday —
There are those who depart
As others just start
With the ride's roundelay —
So I choose a fine horse
For I want to take part
And it bears me away,
Spins past those who leave
And slows to receive
New hands snatching at reins,
Life circling apace in a limited space
To the wistful refrains.
Dear the one by my side
And the loved ones who ride
Through the lengthening day.
But a riderless horse
Keeps its vertical glide
As we circle away.
As the tempo beats slow
Then I suddenly know
That I must alight.
The carousel swings
And the organ still sings
As they spin out of sight.

*First Place Traditional Award 1981*
*National Federation of State Poetry Societies, Inc.*

## With Strings Tied

Emily liked Ezekiel's way
To Heavenly Grace.
He did wheelies in a chariot
That burned through space.
But that was a shade too fast
For Amherst's girl
Fond of the things she would pass
That had made up her world.
So she traded out for a buggy,
With Yankee guile,
And jogged her way to Zion
New England style.

## Confessional

If I could stand upon remembered shore
No path to follow on a trackless sand,
Marking the time, as I was wont before,
Only by birds' home-gatherings on the strand,
And shout into the ocean's whelming roar
All rage toward life, ingested and accrued,
Out-decibeled, 'twould minimize the score
And sum of sin, though payment's overdue.
If I could trace a slow, infilling dawn
Touching a brooding shore and scrubby dune,
Twist naked toes in salty wash along,
My soul and I might yet be God-attuned.

## Odyssey

Walking the high ridge
Of my mind
Trailing a gaunt moon
Cold and alone
With a whistling wind
Bending shadow and silver,
Seeking what I never lost,
Haunted by what I never had.
      My love was sweet
      My love was tall
      I never knew my love at all.

Walking low stretches
That edge the sea
Treading the flat sand
Alone, alone
With the ebbing, flowing tide's
Hushed sound echoing
In the reaches behind my eyes,
Seeking an errant memory,
Something that never happened to me.
      My love was sweet
      My love was tall
      My lover knew me not at all.

## The Enlightened

The apple can be such a devious fruit
As it proved to some kin of mine.
Eve couldn't believe it was meant to deceive
With her eyes of the Innocent Blind.
Delilah's ploy duped a Stupid Boy
In spite of the hosts he slew.
One would think it Plain
To the Simplest Brain
What that Heathen was trying to do!
Yet I who am Wise with wide-open eyes
Still reach for the apple there.
Though a trap be plain to my Clever Brain —
Ah – I find the Philistine fair.

## Backward Slider

To be loved invites temptation
To be wanted works a snare,
Still the pious soul rejects them –
Mine is stern and can forbear.
Loneliness is greater trial:
When I tread a single path
It is with a martyr's smile
I evade the Judgment's wrath.
Yet a simpler thing misleads me –
It has trapped me  many a day –
Boredom teases me to mischief
And I go eagerly astray.

**Legacy**

And what did you get
from the apple, Eve?
Memory, she said,
and words that had yet to be spoken —
pain
and joy
and death.

**Selection**

Lovely once,
She held her age so well
But now, at seventy,
The years have much to tell.
The dress rack held a few
That possibly might do.
She chose defiant red
For courage, so she said.

## Anacahuita

Summer seemed scornful of the arid land
Where hope died softly with the blighted grain.
There hostile winds raked rows with stinging sand
Where cotton dwindled never knowing rain.
The stunted flowers that framed a sagging gate
Made dusty faces in a dry dismay.
Low clouds wrote promise on a sky of slate,
Then tired of teasing took their gifts away.
Where trailing vine and scraggly garden scene
Mutely reproached the stingy, sullen sky,
A miracle of fragrant white and green
Made nothing enough, futility a lie.
Green impudence made ignorance its gain;
It blossomed on when Reason bade it die.
And who survived to taste the tardy rain?
The foolish, stubborn olive tree – and I.

*Anacahuita is the Mexican Olive Tree*

## Serpentes Doggeralis

*(To Dickinson's snake, and D.H.'s snake, add one)*

Of all the trials that I endured
While living on the farm,
The most insoluble of all
Were the rats that ruled the barn.
The rats were small; the rats were tall,
They quite defied us all.

Upright they stood and bared their teeth –
All foes made quick withdrawal.
I brought five cats to quell the rats.
Invincible were they!
Till face to face — cats then with grace
Stayed prudently away.
Two barrels of feed inflamed rat greed
To arrant banditry
Until a guest on rodent quest
Assumed hegemony.
I watched him pour across the floor,
A liquid, languid line,
This lethal king, a slinky friend
Whose appetite was fine.
His barn-width length and sinewy strength
Soon made the rats depart,
Except for those this fellow chose
To dine on a la carte.
This mobile trap incurred the wrath
Of Juan Gutierrez Jones.
Juan's lunch retreat seemed too replete—
He longed to dine alone.

Tortillas fair with stuffings rare
That his noble fare comprised
Weren't tastier, gulped hastier
Beneath a serpent's eye

- - - - - - -

Rats rule again throughout my barn.
My king snake's gone away.
And J. G. Jones looks sinister
When it's mentioned
To this day.
Warm tea and cold tamales –
Who minds the rats at play?

*1952*

*Awarded honorable mention for rhyming poetry competition Writer's Digest #77*

## On Weeping

Weep, for a thing befallen.
Weep, now the thing is known.
Women have wept before you,
And you will not weep alone.

Weep where there's none to hear you;
And weep, if you can, aloud;
For weeping that's done in silence
Weaves the soul an armor — or shroud!

And women will weep tomorrow
For seed that today has sown.
Women will weep, and discover
That in sorrow, their souls have grown.

**Prayer**

Brashly I importuned my Lord,
Expounding need, and citing evidence
My cause was good indeed,
Quoting promises back to Him
Of succor, pastures green,
Defender hosts, invisible about, believing
Almighty God, my claim was just,
Fast forwarded with faith and trust.

But when long waiting did portend
A claim denied, I cried, "Wherefore,"
So sure my Father yet
Would, <u>must</u>, consider more.
And then the answer came: He said,
"You prayed for stones, my child,
I gave you bread."

## Spring Organum

Beneficence of God
falls on wintry ground.
The somber clays grow restless
and aware.
Dark sentient seeds expand
in silent *kyrie*
as deep in earth
the hidden waters rise
in *adoration*.
Mute worms withdraw
from light
leaving their *manifestos*,
*credos* in soil,
pledged in humility.
Green *canticles* compete
declaring *sanctus*
and birds' antiphonies
return the *agnus dei*
for Adam's sin.
Lo, fragrant as God's thought —
Gardens.

*This was an effort to create an extended metaphor. The steps of the Catholic liturgy are incorporated so there is a double entendre.*

**Moonflood**

Moonflood
Bearing the soul
On one sustained and thrumming
Chord
Above the world
Bemused with tranquility,
Fusing with eternity.

O my Soul
Break now the spell
Of the high humming.
Seek dissonance again
And life.

## Long Distance Camera

Vouchsafe no truth,
Catch for us no such image
Of mortality.
Dispassionate as time,
You pictured
The poor, small ape
Who thought the race
Unfair, who never
Chose to run,
Who could but turn
And die.
His glazing eyes reflect
Our terrible cognition,
And we did not know
We knew.
From life's first pulse
We sensed
His questing breath,
Lusting at heel,
Following apace until
One day, brilliant with all life,
Suddenly —
        the Tiger.

**Pavane**

Butterfly wings,
Blithe once, a jeweled flicker
On a flower,
A wayward note afloat
On summer's sweet and shining air,
But faded now, and stiff
In folded stillness,
A fragile prayer

## Death in Mexico

Winter sun
Bright and brittle edged
With sharp and sudden cold,
And from the trees
Like black and orange snowflakes
Falling without sound
They lie in drifts of petals
On the ground.

**Respite**

Never the stuff of sailors
He retreats from the fierce seas,
And so I make him harbor,
Pretending not to see
The bravado in his smile.
Too soon, I know,
He must set forth again
With fear and desperate courage
To dare the storm,
No match for it at all,
And so I bid him go,
Praying my thanks for this brief respite
From the winds that try him so.

## Inland Alien

Haunting, the calls of dove and quail
Drift over me,
    (But the echoing conch of yesterday
      Sings of gulls and sea.)
Whipping the heavy air
The fat doves rise,
    (Gay comics* skim grey scud
      With laughing cries.)
In sandy valley shall I die
Who was born by sea?
How keep death's rectitude
And primly lie
If it call me?

---

*The gulls along the Texas coast are called Laughing Gulls

**Mea Culpa**

I try not to think of Judgment Day;
It promises nothing nice.
If my deeds do not speedily,
Send me Hell's way,
I'm sure that my dreams will suffice.

## Illusion

Walk now with care
Into my waking dream
The cloak I hold for you
Will make you seem
The very giant that I seek
Dreams must be lightly worn
Lest you expose the seam

**Lucifer or Lochinvar!**

Lucifer or Lochinvar?
Ah, neither,
For each would be
Splendid,
In his way
And you were only
Pitiable,
In the end.

## East Texas Morning

The potter turns in his sleep,
moves his legs, tired still
from standing at the wheel
to work the cool red clay
with his soft hands.
Blue jays shrill good mornings
from the great spread oak,
as the crows call from the stern pines.
The clay must wait, shapeless, patient,
for the master's touch
to shape the graceful vessel.
The potter stirs in his sleep.

## Ah, Eve

Where was the sorrow
Of "bringing forth"
When there was the warm joy
Of small mouths
Seeking your breast
And tiny hands
Exploring the world
Outside the garden?
Where was the joy
When you cradled
Abel's head as he lay
Devastated by his brother?
Seth was Seth — not Abel —
Nor was he Cain
Exiled far from your eyes
And heart.
"Bring forth," a finite phrase
Proscribing infinite bondage.

## Hosea's Wife

The cymbals, the seductive bells
      still advertise abandon.
Sweet incense flames the mind
        like that which won you once
        from Piety's close vigilance.
"Abide, Gomer."
        Quiescent, mute,
Rebuke the rebel tendencies,
        your obdurate will abscinded
        by a terrible Grace.
Be isolate!
Bathe the slight wounds with silence.
Learn to endure redemption
        lest you betray the silver
        and set at nought the barley
        an homer —
        and a half.

*Hosea 3:1-3*

**Ezekiel**

In death's dry valley
Bleached bones
Can shake, reverberate and rally,
Touched by an infinite God.

Breathe on the desert heart of me
That I may rise and walk
And be made whole.
Wrap music round my soul,
Like royal robes.
So I, clothed in this loving
Grace from God
May lose earth's stain
And step beyond its bitterness
And pain.

## Sic Transit

Come love with me
And for a space
Be heart to heart
And less alone
Before the sweet
Is memory,
And memory is turned
To stone.

## Nolle Prosequi

I foot-raced against Time
But oh — he won,
For he had reached the end
Before I'd scarce begun.
I wagered against Death,
He laughed aloud.
I seamed a party dress –
He wove a shroud.

## 40 Knots

The wind holds conversation
With my nerves
Parleys along the lining
Of my skull,
Rifles the insulation
Round my thoughts,
Leaving them disarrayed —
So ill-arranged
And different
From what I have allowed
In late considered calm.
How shall I order them,
Again, or touch
The sharp and bitter edges,
Lying unreconciled?

## Eden's Exile

Poor adam
with itching eve-bone
in his breast,
turned from insular one-ness
to the mating quest.
Dumb adam,
gullible fool, who found
weapons to hand,
and thought
he conquered ground.
Lo, adam,
poor stumbler,
only man
waking to meet his mind,
uncharted land.
Self-exiled, maze-wanderer,
seeking still
lost innocence
too long
seduced by will.
Miming potentate
who doesn't know
he's sod,
searching for mini-parity
with God.

## Lot's Wife

The winds of the night blew over me,
Briny, salty, cold,
Breathing soft of a restless sea
Where a moon burned orange-gold.
The past was ashes with Nineveh,
But lured by the plaintive strain
My hands slipped off the plowshare
While my soul looked ... back, again.

*1946*

**Flight To Zion**

Salt monolith, caught out in looking back,
Who called your name?
When bells of pagan temples shrieked
As Jahweh's wrath scourged idols
You walked on, until
The indiscriminate fires
Your homely posts and lintel claimed.
Through tumult, what flickering sound
Impelled you to turn back
Toward Gomorrah?
That wistful look was gulled
By memories unreconciled to ashes.
Transfixed your gaze,
Forever bemused by yesterday
Though its certitudes are sand,
While Lot trudged through mirage
Spit the grit from his teeth,
And wagered for Holy Land.

**The Box**

Bounded by opaque time
that circumscribes brief space
allotted me,
I wait
like Schrodinger's cat
for my observer, God,
not to ask whether I now am dead
but, rather,
Was it I who lived?

## VOWS

A cage there was
that spacious seemed, and wide.
The flowers, a few, belied
the gate of iron that closed,
and I, inside.

**Accounting**

I found you lying as at rest
In cool, serene disdain,
No sigh or show.
In quiet vehemence
You took the spark of life
And snuffed it out,
(Great God!—
As if you knew
What Death was all about!)
Reduced God's Will
To such little scope
That one small vial
Could order it,
Giving life back just
Casually,
An act deemed worth
The Hell
Ledgered perhaps to you,
Not reckoning the sum
Bequeathed to me.

**Impotence**

While I lay dreaming, someone died.
I lifted up my face to sun
All unaware it also warmed
A far, devouring tide.
There was no chance to contest
With the sea, although its prize
Was irreplaceable to me.
How can love even hope
To neutralize, afar, a caustic grief,
Or yearning annul
The wound's dark cicatrix
That presages a scar?
Where is the strategy, in afterthought,
To counter harm? What good
The sentinel shout, summoning love
To arm, within the citadel,
When all the vulnerable
Are ranged so far without?

## For Crying Out Loud

"For crying out loud," he said
And she replied,
"I wouldn't think of it.
I cry quite neatly
Deep inside."

**Façade**

Sleepless I rise,
I bathe, I dress,
I smile, I drive,
I work, I speak,
I smile
The while, inside my head,
someone is praying, weeping,
    screaming
      screaming
        screaming

## Dialogue

Somewhere beyond time,
Mother mine,
I would like to talk to you.
    So many things
    I never asked,
    So many things
    I never knew.

Somewhere beyond time,
Daughter mine,
Would you like to talk to me?
    So many things
    I could never do —
    So many things
    I could never be.

**Summation**

So many pieces of me
Strewn along the way
Organic, spiritual, intellectual detritus.
Some well lost,
And I the better for it.
Others, had they lingered —
Perchance
Remnants subtly
Conceiving serenity.

## Stones from the Jordan

Oh, God, as my heart kneels
beside these stones of memory,
wet still from the Jordan of my life,
stained by the times I strayed,
the times I failed,
they testify of blessing, undeserved,
yet shining through your Mercy, Lord,
      your Love.
O Father God, grant my children
kneeling beside their stones of memory,
shall know You and your Grace,
and make an altar
for their healing place.

*Joshua, Chapter 4*

**Impasse**

I would reject
That souls incarnate in this flesh
Emerge incarnadined,
That flesh in stoic sympathy
Craves re-assimilation
With the dust,
Until I feel my life's dynamic thrust
Snared in minutiae.
Life's inertia is
Death's surrogate,
A mockery to harass mankind.
Bitter the resistance
Which turns the most
Fastidious and sanguine
Into the soul's philosophy
"Better another's crucifix than mine."

**Passage**

Sometimes man dies
Because it makes a difference
Sometimes
Because it will make
No difference.
In the black night of despair
Love calls not —
Sleep comes not —
And Death
Inchworms closer
In sure
Sly increments.

## Lonely Places

Earth covets dark and lonely places
Where raptors wings slice
Through brooding skies,
Silent hunters stalking
Soft foragers, trembling
At stray sound,
For hunger knows no pity
When hapless prey are found.

Black night shrouds the great city
Stone walls border dark alleys
Offering no shelter.
Soft hiss of brakes,
And a tired night worker
Exits a lumbering bus.
Soft pools of light mark dark stretches.
Rapacious eyes assess the distance
To warmth and safety
Of a waiting door.

**Discards**

I hoarded dreams
against the day when, freed,
I'd take them out
and live them, one by one.
At last the gate swung wide
and making haste I fled
away from bondage, clutching
my bag of dreams.

At safe remove, I took them out
and, every one, examined them anew.
These were the young girl's dreams,
this the young woman's dearest wish,
And here the matron's deep desires,
entities remembered with a faint familiarity,
But I am none of these.
Such dreams were conjured
by extinguished fires.
Would someone take them,
Please?

**The Unburdened**

But bones and stones
Those I have laid away
Who once seemed so like
Crosses to be borne.
Why do I miss
Accustomed weight, today,
And keep the road to memory
So worn?

**Reckoning**

How did the days run down
   to the few that are left to me?
Why is the path grown strange along
   the edge of the westward sea?
Where is the girl that I left behind
   that I always thought I'd be?

Where was the gate that opened in
   on a place my own?
Which was the door to enclose my space
   when the day had gone?
Whose was the heart that was mine to keep
   as the years rolled on?

**Nightfall**

How quickly the darkness falls this time of year,
    with such a final feel,
    a curtain quickly drawn
    on winter's shortening days.
Names echo in my mind like motes
    swirling within the rays of slanting light,
    snippets of a song
    that once I sang in full.
    Soft fragments linger in my memory.
Night falls, scattering the motes
Among them — mine.

**Disconnect**

Another line is dead.
Another voice is disconnected
With no call forwarding
Across the timeless void.
How I wander
The echoing halls of memory
To seek an unlisted number.

## At A Grave

Gold ... where the rays of sunlight
    are dying against my door.
Gold leaves trace a summer
    fading into a nevermore ...
Gold, the ribbon
    that binds red roses
    where a heart was buried
        so long before .....

## The Delivery

The shrouded days go by
like guilty penitents,
pausing to leave a knotted sack
outside my door
for me to heave upon a back
already sore.
Ah once, a better time,
you left a lighter load
and I see well that even gifts
are left for some.
But now, a few doors down,
a grim, dark bag that trifles mine?
Yes, leave my heavy sack.
It is a timely fit for I have still
a tender back, and I must try
to lean into the weight
and toughen it against the day,
that bitter day, it is for me
you bring the black bag by.

**Roses**

At one o'clock, it seems
I woke from fitful dreams
To think that once upon a time
And far away, I could grow roses.
I had a home, I had a yard
And I grew roses.

This place I have, these pleasant rooms,
Suffice for me.
I neither groom nor spray
To coax the lovely blooms.
The house, the yard
Now shelter someone else,
And I am blessed by what I have.
But once upon a time,
One soft, remembered yesterday,
I did grow roses.

## Durable Foe

On garden path of stones
the tell-tale passage of my foe
has left a silver trail –
the slow and patient snail.
I spread the lethal granules everywhere
with care, to save spring's loveliness
from moonlight depredations,
counting the tale of vanquished shells
with my unkind elation.
Yet I know well that when, at last,
I shall reside beneath a stone,
bathed in night's soft light
the gleaming trail, still silver, etched
across that stone, will note my ire
did not prevail against the pale
translucent snail.

*Houston 1998*

## The Challenge

For thoughts that glitter
When exposed to light,
Fracturing to shards
The brittle and confining molds,
Ask.

For mysteries hidden
Behind great doors
Turning on ancient hinges,
Seek.

For ways man yet
May travel
To circumnavigate
The far wilderness
Of his soul,
Knock.

Yea,
Rattle the very gates
Of heaven.

## Of Saints and Sinners, Mostly Sinners

Born to a world
Perpetually unready;
Small wonder
That the face
Is wrinkled
In a cry.
Modest enigma
Wrapped in blue
With hands
Close clenched
Upon a secret.
Will he be saint
Or sinner? Both,
No doubt, and
Well enough.
The world can bear
Few sinners,
Absolute, and living saints
Prefers to do
Without.

## The Tally

Here count one, Census Taker,
Only one,
And one day slow to come
Count none.
This house was full before,
So many empty days ago.
I get a letter, sometimes,
Full of busy ... sorry ... soon ...
Their pictures smile there vaguely,
Always looking past me.
Count me here and now.

Count on, count on,
In small, decrepit frame, count one.
In dingy flat, count one.
In rented room, count one.
In nursing home, count one,
Count many ones.
And then one day,
Count just a cypher less
Among the many cyphers more,
Subtracting naught from anyone,
Not even me, for I
Am the one dying
Among the already dead.

*1962*

*Faith became a census taker in 1960.*

## The Valley Boy's Homecoming

The winter sun allows a muted warmth
To land which, come July,
It scorches vehemently.
Mantilla'd in black,
She seems so small, discomfited
Before the officer's gravity and strength.
She takes the flag he proffers, folded precisely.
Earth's old priority has claimed the firstborn son.
Clutching the rosary she evokes another time —

   Other brown babies had followed Juan
   And suddenly he was tall before her eyes,
   Strange and beautiful, wearing the uniform ...
   Juan working the endless cotton rows,
   Ignoring the heat that smote at once
   From overhead, and from the burning soil.
   Then, with more money than he had ever known,
   Bound for the small cantinas, and the girls.
   The cotton again will open cushiony squares
   And brown hands reach for it.
   The small cantina will revive, jubilant with accordion
   And guitars, exulting away the night ...

Confused, she stands before official deference.
How far the Rio Grande from Viet Nam?
How far Juan?

**After The Blake Exam**

Little test, I took thee.
Little test, I took thee.
Essays, match-ups, tried them all —
Some I scarcely could recall.
Was he once a gentle fellow
Education did not mellow?
If I get a Ph.D.,
Will it make a Hyde of me?
(But he will have to grade thee.
I'm glad he has to grade thee.)

## Le Professeur

Professor Tedium N. Tweedledee,
He sat upon a chair,
And scattered knowledge
Prodigally
On students everywhere.
As *analogue* was analyzed
It was a thrill
To me.
All learning grew
Apocryphal
And dwindled
Splendidly.

## Number Twenty-One

In English, how useful
the good letter *u*
as often a beginning
(to mention a few:
*u*ltimate, *u*rgent and
*u*biquitous, too.)
'tis seldom an ending,
(though important to yo*u*.)
Of the twenty-six letters
the quaint letter *q*
just can't do without it,
(though a squabble in Scrabble
draws a point, maybe two.)

## The Happy Boys

The boy and the horse
stand, close,
the horse nuzzling the small hand
that smells of range cubes,
and the horse smells like happiness
to the boy.

For one long, shining afternoon
life will stretch outward
forever, for them,
like a green pasture
beside a running stream.

The scrawny Viet Cong crouches
on bandy legs
beside the foreign soldier
who neither knows, nor cares.
Happiness is a shiny watch,
loot claimed from death,
treasure from the steaming mud
beside a stagnant stream.

*1966*

**Barren**

Lord, how shall I
Bring forth bright blossoms
In the desert
Of my soul?
Time has taken my flowers,
My songs.
There is only the scorching sand,
The broken lute.

## Silent Witnesses

Words fall down the page
Vivid, jostling, staccato
With disconnects and overruns,
Urgent
A bitter testament
Desolate.
Riotous often,
Irreverent sometimes
Seeking always,
Poverty of the hope starved heart
Scar tissue of the soul,
Taunting devils
Ever at the ready
To exploit the small mistake,
The painful doubt.
Your seeking to justify
What you perceived as wrongs
That you had done,
When surely you were the one more
Sinned against than sinning.

I do not write these lines.
I am but the scribe
Discerning them
Among your words
That yearned to say
What you could not,

Longing and broken dreams and spirit's quest
These pleas that leaked between the strands
Like silent witnesses
Against us all
Who loved you
But did not hear,
A way to parry hostile circumstance
Negotiate a deal
To yet survive
Into a future increasingly unreal,
Stingy with promise.

Where do you walk now
That you've left this earth?
Does my profound sorrow touch you?
Does my deep love reach you?
Do my prayers follow you?
I long to see brown eyes again.

God grant your advocate
Is One who knows the grievous wounds
That make Death seem a sweet release.
God grant that angels waited there
To take you home,
To love and joy and peace.

## Deprivation

Few mourn the demise
of forlorn ravens;
some yet reserve lyrics
of old nightingales
for wayward dreams;
many applaud
caustic commentaries
of bright and specious
mockingbirds;
but oh, the prolonged paucity
of thrushes,
singing,
is cause enough
for sackcloth,
for ashes.

**Solitary Night-Shift Man**

The afternoon peaks high
He rises from his bed,
Adjusts his day attire — his outer self,
Impermeable, he goes
Into the world of others,
Behind a calculated mien.
He does life's necessary things
With careful, studied grace.
After each small transaction,
He goes his way, this quiet man,
And later, those he saw
Can scarce recall his face.
Day fades ...
At work he does his portion
Well enough.
Night wanes; his labor done,
He turns to home,
For such he deems the simple,
Private rented space.
He hangs the fabricated outer-self
Upon a hook,
Checks television news,
Its flickering faces.
Heavy drapes drawn against
The waking life outside,
He puts his loneliness to bed.

**The Slow One**

So vulnerable is hope,
and indiscreet;
Wary persistence has
the surer feet.
So perishable, the wistful dream,
while brash surmise,
impatient of ladder, leaps
to claim the skies.
Still, hand over hand, I verify
each rung, and every reach
so carefully rehearse,
nor count it done until the topmost one,
Earth-tethered still, but craving
Universe.

**riddle**

if all the "if only's"
became "were's,"
could they erase
Golgotha?
transmute one rack
into a resting place?
or would new-grown "however's"
re-arrange the score
and add to rows of crosses
many more?

**Confrontation**

The quality
of grief erodes
the fatuous pretense
that screens
the fallible heart
and leaves
no hiding place.

## Loren Eiseley

I cannot say in what far place
this man may be.
I could not cite the color of his eyes,
or ever know his voice,
or see his face.
But, oh, his words leap living
from the page,
as down strange paths
they lead me on.
Pursue the winged thoughts,
scientist, mystic, and
we will hoard them as
found treasure, and follow
as you 'let the red fox run.'

**Et je rapelle**

Snow! — this morning
Feathers falling soundlessly
From close grey skies.
And what is left to tell of beauty now?
A ragged edge that lies
Along the garden path — forgotten —
Bordering icy stones along
Like piles of dirty cotton ...

*1942-The first time to see snow*

**Rain**

The land thirsts,
Grimaces,
In dry, cracked smiles
And then, dissolves
In rain, and
Populates
With instant frogs
And shrieking children
Seeking puddles.

## Spring Rain

The spring's first rain calls softly
To silent, wintered ground,
Urging a green renewal
With pleading sound.

I feel the earth awaken
Like a resurrected thing;
And my own heart is shaken
To think of spring.

The earth has had enough of rest.
Life rises from her sod
To wait and hope, to weep and sing,
To testify of God.

**July in Houston**

And summer ripens,
Comments daily in the rasp
Of oversized magnolia leaves,
Brown, brittle, blown
By the hot wind
Across baked concrete

## Mowing In Summer

The smell of childhood
essence of growth
with long grass falling
to the sharpened blades,
yielding odours of sunshine
recalling the verdant spring
today's green dissipated
in shimmering noons.

## June of '67

Dubious contest, to pit a giant
Against a simple shepherd boy, until
The stone flew,
Catching the giant square
So that he stood uncertainly,
In stunned surprise,
Before he fell.
Peacekeepers stood aghast
And then demanded that
David un-throw that stone,
Take it back
Into his sling, but this
Was hard to do, for
Goliath lay there, fallen
To the dust of the earth.

*Written following the Six Days War*

**Mirror**

My errands done, I have arrived at home
(or such I call it now),
And, in my head, I cry, "Hello, I'm home."
(It seems I should announce that I am here.)
"Hello, I'm home."

The walls accept my salutations
But silent stand, and I provide
The only movement anywhere, I see.
A single face
Returns my hopeful gaze,
Reflection in a mirror — me.

## Child of Mine

If winter goes, and spring should come
To find me here without you,
Then there could be no recompense for me
What good to celebrate the spring
If you were gone?

But when spring comes
And I'm no longer here,
Take joy in everything God gives
Whatever blooms or sings,
Immortal music made by mortal man —
This I have done, so long as you are here.

## Victory Sonnet

The dying sun retreats beyond the hill,
And there is barely light to catch the prize.
Weary, past joy, I claim the finish line,
Hills too painfully traversed to itemize,
Declare these valleys and those meadows owned
And all the vistas once beyond my ken,
The running years defied, for I have won.
Full circle home, I turn my steps again.
But where are those who sent me on my way,
And dared me on to race against the sun?
Gone? How gone, since yesterday?
Shout after them the sum of all I've done!
        Faintly returns my toll of metes and bounds
        From some conclusive barrier to sound.

*1967-"When I finally got my degree, both my parents were gone."*

## On Making Poetry

Among slow-minted coins
A few doubloons,
Some counterfeits,
And large
Mexican centavos,
Weighty,
With little purchase power,
And even, sometimes,
Gold ones,
Possibly pilfered.

## Bio: Faith Patricia Williams Ingle Collins

Born October 10, 1921- Corpus Christi, Texas
Died March 22, 2013- Round Rock, Texas

She was a child of the Depression, raised by uneducated parents. During years of separation from her husband during WWII, she began to write of her life. He was a bomber pilot and returned home suffering from PTSD, unknown and undiagnosed in those times. He chose to try farming, which forced her into an isolated life punctuated by mental, emotional and physical strain. She continued to write during hardscrabble times made worse by a long-term drought in the 1950s.

After they moved back to Corpus Christi she earned her Associate's Degree from Del Mar College in 1957. At 45 years of age she completed Texas A & I in Kingsville, Texas, as valedictorian with a perfect 4.0, despite being required to take swimming, which she hated. A & I is now part of the University of Texas system. She then earned a Master's Degree in English, also from Texas A & I. She studied Library Science at the University of Texas.

Faith was an English teacher, and after remarriage and a move to Houston became a proposal writer for Houston Independent School District. She traveled extensively all over the British Isles, Europe, Spain, the Netherlands, New Zealand, Canada and the United States. After her first retirement she was a grant writer for Communities in Schools. At 75, after her second retirement, she moved to Round Rock. Faith enjoyed reading, painting, writing, and keeping in touch with her five children and the rest of her large family.

Her work has been seen infrequently by the public before this printing, but when shown has won accolades. However, it is well known and loved by her progeny. Her inspiration, encouragement, and reviews of her offsprings' work were desired and dreaded, for her honesty in criticism was unflinching and never colored by her affection.

# MY DAUGHTER

## Love and Dirt

### Laura McCarty

## Map of the World

I spread the map across the table,
smoothing out the folds
to measure the distance between us.

My thumb and index finger travel the miles
in inches as I scale mountains to move closer to you.
The solitude I feel from the vast blue
that separates us
retreats
as I follow the lines of ocean currents
toward your land.

New shores bring me new explorations
as my thumb and finger now crawl their way
over the expansiveness of your chest.

As I spread my arms out wide like wings
and flatten myself into the creases of you
the heavy weight of my heart releases its baggage.

You grip my sides
and then fold your arms
around me.
The distance disappears
as you close the map
and carry me home.

## The Caretaker

I walk behind you from stone to stone
as you drag the garden hose through the maze.
The water soaks the ground and forms a river.

You point to one flower and then another
and rattle off Latin names,
"Hyacinthus orientalis."

"Say it again, Grandmother."
"Sugar, call me Lucy Lee."

I follow you on hands and knees
as you dig and plant seeds for autumn.
Later, you pull me in the faded-red wagon
and we move piles of dirt together.

Twenty years gone and I drive you now
to visit your vacant home.
We walk in the garden among the steady growth
of weeds and flowers unattended.

A cane supports your ageing frame
when you stop to ask which of those are in bloom
because your sight is failing.
But the names, I cannot remember.

I know only to take the leaves from the fish pond
before the goldies suffocate,
put water in the birdbath because it has not rained.
The flowers I abandon.

You wither now on a hospital mattress
Surrounded by metal bars that move
up and down, from chair to bed.

Your calloused hands from years of tending,
clutch me
when you tell me not to bury you
in a steel casket, only wood,
so you can feed the flowers.

"Not deep," you whisper.
"I want to breathe into my azaleas."

I place you in the ground
where your flowers can stand in the sunshine.
Violet and red.

## I dislocated my heart to silence the belly of my soul
(for Edgar Allan Poe)

First it was the shower head's
drip against the chrome. I turned
the reflecting handle until my knuckles were white.
I shut the bathroom door and locked myself in the bedroom,
but its annoying rhythm seeped
through the walls. Its pings spurred me
to smash the faucet with the sledge hammer
I found in the garage.

But then it was the second hand tick
from my watch across the room.
I can't be blamed for the interruptions
it caused. I hid time beneath stacks of clothes
to smother the harmony. I buried myself
under pillows and sheets,
but the infinite seconds could be heard.

The unremitting beat encouraged me
to pull a high heel from my closet and bang
against its shiny, numberless face. The glass cracked
and I pulled its rotating hand from the body
and threw it to the ground.

By three a.m. I had stripped
my house of vibrations and repetitions,
but again I could hear an echoing
throb inside my head. I reached
down my throat scraping my hand against pearly teeth
and ripped the pitter patter from its source.

Clenching the organ between my fingers
I could feel the pulse in my palm.
I squeezed harder, emptying the artery until flutters ceased.

I rolled over in my skin to escape
the odor and last decaying twangs.
I had bled the world free of sound.

*Published in the spring of 1993 in the* GW Review.

## Turning the Dirt

Every August evening
the neighbors watch
me in the garden, digging
and mumbling curses at the cat
that defecates on my flowers.

The two 80-year-old sisters
peer from their lace curtains
while I crouch on my knees clipping
back my roses hours after sunset.

I hide in the bushes when I hear
their screen door scratch open
to avoid making excuses
for my absence at church.

But the ladies see me by the moon
that exposes my ripened face, smudged
with dirt from my garden gloves.
My hair pinned up in tangles,
makes the creases around my eyes seem deeper,
embedded.

Previous days of sunlight have blotched
my shoulders with freckles
where the sundress missed.

As I spring from the hedges
to chase the black squirrels
from my marigolds and pick the dead

locust out of my soil, I notice
the abundance of overgrown impatiens.

Dodging the weeds,
I strangle their thin spines
rip their skinny bodies from the dry
earth and tightly wind each around
my fingers like old string.

I pull each white petal
from its body.

Limb by limb,
I crumble to the ground.

Beneath the poison moonlight
I wilt and bury myself
in the bed of my garden.

## The Placid Warrior

Three crows circle you over Manassas
with the indigo backdrop
as your battleground.

The black birds caw at you,
fierce warrior,
but you do not retreat.

Hovered above unmarked graves
of decaying bones
you smell the buried soldiers
long since dead.
Your senses tell you
that bodies doused in blood
have sunk, coloring the soil a deeper brown.

The crows seek warfare on your snowy tips,
but you refuse to engage.
The smaller birds capture you in their circle,
pluck at your beady eyes
and destroy your x-ray vision.

The dead leaves tease you now
as they crimson red on the October ground.
You disappear in the harvest sun
and escape their violent sport.

In the naked sky, wings full out,
hook beak pointed down,
you expose your tender breast
and storm the earth.

**Journey**

Your small notebook
that flips over
instead of to the side
sits in the empty seat
with your black fine pen
tucked through its broken spiral rings.

You wear your green cap backwards
with your "holy" red and white jersey.
The open window colors your left arm.

Sun bolts in the rearview mirror
block your vision.
You wince as I stand
watching you
waving in the drive.

## Observatory Place

They told me spring was to come
so I stayed with elbows crunched
in grass that left mazes on my skin.

My hands held my head and shoved
cheeks into my eyes as I looked
for billboard signs
alerting its arrival.

And I waited while sweat
exuded from the separation
of my breasts and rays
whitened my hair.

From winter to summer
someone forgot the cool
evenings and morning dews.

In anticipation I readied
my garden, planting
pansies and petunias, too.
But my impatiens wilted and burned.

Resting on clovers and weeds
I searched for the not-so-scorching sun
while watching Mrs. Kepheart
clip her unbudded roses
and Mr. Coyne play dominoes
from almost white wicker
and worn daisy cushions.

Down my street
from porch to porch
I patiently observed us all
waiting for those few weeks
they call spring.

**The Weight of You**

I've forgotten if it's the hairs on your chest
the length of your arm
or the weight of you
that I miss.

In the dark,
I let the moon carry you back
on her electric beams.
Her shadows create shapes I imagine
are your arms and legs.

I've forgotten if it's the sound of your heels
clicking against the sidewalk
or the lengthy silences
between your breaths.

We stand at the window
wrapping ourselves
in the curtains like sheets,
our bodies defined
but changing with our movements.

I've forgotten if it's the way
you fasten my glass beads
zipper my dress
or trace my curves with your fingers.

We pull the heavy fabric from its rod
and collapse to the wooden floor.

I've forgotten if it's the smell of your shoes,
your shirts after a day of work.

Our bodies entwined we watch the moon
shroud herself, taking her light with her.

I've forgotten you.

## To Maya

Maya! You made me richer.
You rushed me
to song,
to sorrow,
to joy.

Goodbye, teacher.
I know you will not rest,
but may your found peace in life
continue in death.
May your words be louder now,
your smile remembered.
Sing!

**Story on the Rim**

I'm stark on this copy block,
rigid, pale, with my printed
letters freezing on the galley.

My words are interpreted as factual.
Lines reflect only my eyes
not my soul.

I search for a different truth
where beauty converts to puffery.
My pad lacks adjectives, adverbs.
Descriptions seem too biased or vague.

I clock out inches and dead__lines.
Deceptive politicians and money mongers
are to intrigue me
not cut grass or purple sunsets.

At one a.m. in the smoked-out
newsroom among coffee-stained mugs
my computer terminal reflects
a face —

A story with a great head ...
"Poet dies of suffocation."

## Saturday Chores

She loosened stuck lips
from blue wool scarf strings
and knocked grey slush from her
genuine imitation Chilean toast boots.

Her frozen vinyl mittens stood straight
on ribbed rubber thawing beneath her feet.
Chicago's L-heater clanked,
puffing on and off tepid air,
chapping cheeks exposed
to heavy, slimed, exhausted gusts pouring in
between slaps of train doors each stop.

She pulled November's *Redbook*
from her brown papered groceries,
chomping Freedent gum.
Reading twenty ways to keep inches off
she dove into her purse
for the gum's foil wrapping to save for later.

Dentures fresh, she delved
into chocolate cherry creams,
wiping mouth clean with her now soggy scarf.
Saturday's ride shook her through buildings,
forcing her size 16 stomach to split
her poly-cotton panel pants.

Poking umber eyes out from her purple fur hat,
she laughed aloud watching her stop go by.

## Painted Woman/Painted Fathers

Momma's torn laced nightgown
slides over her breasts
as she shifts in the polyester.

She fingers the rat's nest
in my wheat strands
hoping I won't ask to hear the same stories.

"He's the dustman wiping his brow,
dragging his stallion through town
while a toothpick wrestles with dinner.

"He curtains his scarlet hair beneath a fedora.
His Burberry screams his pride
strutting by way of New York.

"He cuddles the clown's red button,
dancing on carnival grounds.
It is the treasured ruby begonia.

"He is a feeble old-timer rocking
on the veranda browsing through yellow
photos with his long-worked leathered hands."

She pulls my hair aside leaving
russet silk lip stamps on my cheeks.
I always wait for Momma's kiss good night.

**Brief Sensations**

Aged fish reeks violently up
from your basketball shoes.

Salty sweat splatters on my Spic-n-Span
tablecloth-sized floor. You squeak by,

bouncing rubber on our carpet
and Mrs. Crowe's ceiling. Your moist

dripping clothes smother me
in your grip before your shower.

Trickles of rusted water heighten
the ankle-deep clogged tub even before lathering.

Three Elvis Costello songs later, you smell
from our Holiday Inn personal soap bars.

## Listening to Kuwait

I pull up to the curb and slide into park.
The radio crackles, fading in and out
as I press my ear against the dashboard.

"Bombs like fireworks. It looks like the
Fourth of July," the broadcaster cries.
His voice quivers,
not the usual reporter's monotones.
"Gasmasks cover tiny faces,
lit clouds hover in the bleak sky.
Buildings crumble from sudden jolts
in the earth.
Bolted, taped doors and windows flap
like paper in a windstorm.
The sky and ground are now a cruel black.
The barbed wire encloses the city and
invites bullets and bombs to explode."

I hear them scream. Panicked voices vanish.

I glance to my house lit up by the corner lamp.
My ear, turned sideways, waits to hear
the next radio wave.
My safety belt is still fastened.

*Jan 1991*

**Texas Tunes**

Stuffed between four Fords at the stoplight
*Amarillo by Morning* plays on truck radios.

With windows down, I raise my frequency,
humming Italian sounds.
Pavarotti and I now scream over George Strait.

I silence the crowded intersection.

I check lip lines and lick
my spotted pink teeth.

My side-mirror catches
disapproving cowboy glares.

The light turns green;
I grip the wheel,
adjust my seat and drive.

## Meet Me Beneath the Sitka Spruce

The metropolitan summer odor wakes me
from my dreams of you,
you, beneath a black sky
spotted with Oregon stars.

Here, behind these urban walls
I am braced in shackles,
jailed from touching your face.
I see your figure in my window panes.

I lift my head from the pillow
to meet you,
but my body sticks to the bed.

I allow the morning heat to melt my skin
from its muscles, shed my ligaments
and tendons from the bone
and disintegrate my marrow
and organs to ashes.

I take shape in the western air
and wait for the mending of hearts
beneath a Sitka spruce.

**Reoccurring**

Back pains remind me of Saturdays.

Hotel room floors return the burns to my thighs.
Window screens resemble his pocked, crusty face.

Fat hands force me to hide my wrists in coat pockets.
Scabby knees bring back bruises to my stomach.
Rain mildew perspires his cheap Black Flag cologne.

Missing buttons and broken zippers leave me shaking.
Blue tattoos draw sweat from my eyes in my nightmares.

The letters that spell his name force me to rip
Nails in clenched teeth.
Sex now haunts me
As his stale lingering secretion exposes me.

Morning rays wake me
And every day I plot.

## Peach Colored Pills

Green eyes fixed on the oval shape
she rubs her lower stomach
with a different stroke.

Over the morning Formica counter
she reaches for the peach colored pills.
She removes the grey plastic
popping one out
of its hole.

Tightly turning it between thumb and finger
she pauses then swallows without juice
creating an invisible lump
in her throat.

Designs on her forehead today
are creases tomorrow.

One less or one lost child for her to bear.

## The Fig Thief

With a glance back to the main house
where guides lead visitors through the stately grounds
we walk backwards briefly then turn to flee.

Breaking from the cameras and talking noise
we sprint down the hill to Monticello's orchards
and like Dionysius we discover
rows of Marseilles fig trees blooming.

In the June heat that hangs in the air
I watch you steal from the trees
that have escaped the Christian curse.
"Eat these quickly,"
you demand
and gift three to me.

With one bite, our innocence melts
as I imagined it did for Sally Hemmings,
when she spread herself beneath the branches,
forced or welcomed, maybe both,
like a child emerging from the womb,
and passed from girl to woman.

What secrets live in those boughs from now
and centuries ago
under layers of leaves, bark and color
is our truth and freedom alone.

Is it blood or is it juice
spilling from the red flesh inside the fruit

that you lick from my fingers
giving us the taste of pleasure
for pleasure's sake.

Under the microscope of gaggling ladies and politicians,
I suspect she conceded to her lover's pleas
that others called bargains
to live a life of slavery, to live a life with him.

Some say owned, I say loved, for I know the shackles
that bind us when the heart is open but not broken.
You are my master as I am yours.
Equal in love, no words of the populace can determine
right from wrong
Like the gossip these two swallowed for 38 years,
the seeds catch in our teeth,
but we do not spit any out.

Instead we consume history
and hide the evidence of our theft.
In return, no thunderbolts are thrown our way by Jupiter.
Perhaps now — as then — in these fields of fruit
unseen crimes can be forgiven.

Sweet sugar eaten, we run for the shuttle bus
that will take us down the lane
that grows grass in gravel
but not guilt
for curses and supposed-sins do not wither
nor destroy
what God deems just.

## New Orleans Goodbye

Sunglasses slide off my nose
as sweat forms between my thighs
and a film surfaces on my teeth.

My black patent pumps sink
in the mud quickly, and drops roll from my armpits.

I slide my hand across the cold marble
fingering the etchings of your name.

Aunt Mildred with her colossal bug eyes
and electric blue wig
leans against the gravestone wall
gasping about the heat.

Little Jimmy shovels stolen finger doughnuts
from pockets to mouth,
facing the priest.
Father Daniel sprays his holy water
with a communal chant.

"Receive her Lord and present her to the highest."

Breathing these words, I apologize to you, dear Vera
as my mind tunes out.

I want to dance on the stones
with the black children twirling their mourning umbrellas.

Heels sinking deeper now, I can only wonder
did I turn off the water
or will I return to a flooded yard?

**Fly By Love**

Your sleek black cycle parked with the nose out
was simply waiting for us.

I didn't know you but asked you for a ride.
With ease and without questions
you handed me your jacket
and fastened your helmet on me.

I straddled myself over the fender,
locking arms around you.

You pulled me closer and told me to hold on tight.

I pressed my breasts against you,
swallowing the space between us.

You fell into my lap as we flew through the traffic,
leaving behind our children, our names.

For 15 minutes, we stole from others
and called it our own.

I let your smell become my smell
as we traveled together,
zigzagging across yellow lines.

You leaned back into me.

My head fit against your shoulder.
And we smiled.

## Radiology

The man in white straps
my arms to my chest
ordering me to stillness and leaves me
beneath this tunnel.
He pushes the button for music
to soothe my nerves.
The Japanese violins play
slightly louder in my ears
than the radioactive clicks.

Dressed in aqua-green
the robe exposes my back
to gleaming, slick metal.
My legs begin to shake,
the pounding my heels
create hovers only in my head.
Deep in the tube,
bare feet turn yellow
with purple spots icing over.

Locked in, barred from scratching,
the itch on my chin confines me more.

I crunch teeth together,
dig nails into my palms
and bury my screams.
Over my breasts
I stretch to see the tips of my toes.
My back waits to twist,
crack.

Strings and bows struggle in the air,
echoing off empty walls.
Lying on the MRI platform,
I wait holding my breath.

**Morning Surprise**

Tuesday night
around three
silent sirens
erased my REMs.

Outside the window
flashing shadows
circled my bare
pale yellow walls.

Broken headlights
and pukey orange
paint chips crushed
beneath paramedics' black soles.

Bent guardrails
and brown spots
on the grey street blinded
under neon bulbs.

Ignoring the ruckus
I tangled my legs
in clean sheets hoping
the Valium would set in.

Wednesday morning
Dr. Whigham's class
dozed me through
Gullliver's Travels.

Twenty minutes into Lilliput
the TA interrupted
my needed sleep, handing
me a crumpled letter.

Flattening the cotton
fiber I scanned
the list sloppily
so I could resume my dreams.

Guadalupe often left
cold names
of people unknown
to me.

But you were number six.
Damn it!
Why did you die
outside my window?

**Sometimes**

Sometimes
in the afternoons
I climb back into bed
and lay myself exactly to you
to your shape and your body indentations
on the sheets
that I refuse to change.

I sometimes
bury my nose in your shirts
and hide on the floor of your closet
when the children are gone at school.

I sit at your desk, sometimes,
wear your glasses and imagine
how your black and almond-shaped eyes still see me.

Sometimes
I write you letters and reply to myself.
You tell me you love me. And I know it's true.

Years after you left
I sometimes cursed God for loving you
more than myself.

All the time
I remember you
standing on the platform
snow falling
just before the train took you away
as your body is dragged across the tracks.

I see you always
briefcase and book flying in the air,
looking back at me.

Sometimes
I jump, too.

**Blessed Curse**

Life giving, tender
security
firm, full, flat, flabby, fatty
white, dark, red, bumpy, smooth
milky nutrition.

Innocent until the monster
strikes seeking to kill.
One lump or two?

My sweet, soft, nursing bosom scalpel'd
left only to the slow song of death.

**Viens à moi**

Viens à moi dans l'obscurité de la nuit
et vole-moi de ma personne secrète.

Come to me in the dark of the night
and steal me from my secret self.

## I don't think swings were made for women's hips

I squeezed myself inside the rubber swing
And pushed back with my feet.
Within seconds my shoes were kicking the sky.
My knee joints creaked with every bend,
But I still swung, pulling the set from the ground.

The gravity from my heavy cheeks, yanked me back,
Prohibiting my full rotation.
The metal ropes swallowed my legs,
Leaving chain marks on my thighs.
I hoisted my butt up and leaped to the sand.
I landed with my mouth fighting grains of dirt.
Grit creviced between my teeth
And inflicted pain on my swelling gums.

Around my crow's feet
Tears turned brown powder to mud.
I stood to shake my clothes
And inspect my breasts and not-so-skinny thighs.

I was shocked to find my body was no longer fifteen.

## Before the morning rises

We walk to the beach's end
to meet the roar of the Pacific's current
that shoots floating logs back to shore.

These barkless trees, bleached by sun and water,
bury themselves in the deep of the sand
like dinosaur bones.

Facing the body of water in the cold mist
we are left alone.

Together.

We shear each layer of wool
expose our winter skins
and let the chilling water lap between our toes.
Our feet drag leaving for a moment
our presence in the sand.

In a victory stance our hands clasp
and raise as we approach the ocean's darkness
side by side.

I look above our heads to see my thin, white hand
wrapped by your great, darker palm
as the rising and retreating waves
paste salt to our legs.

In our gentle grasp we walk deeper
and greet the day.

## The Benediction

You scream and pound
your fists on the wooden pulpit.
Your eyes begin to bleed
and I concentrate on your victims.

They shift on red,
plush velvet cushions
that slide across the pew
squeaking, crushing.

Mrs. Didier flips through
Matthew, Mark, Luke and John
searching for passages
similar to those you preach.

Her feathered Sunday hat blocks your face.
So I listen to the inflections
your voice penetrates.

Mother dotes on you,
nodding with your every verse,

Into a "world without end. Amen. Amen."

Your hand raises, palm out against the air
barring evils, forcing them to repel
or roll off.

Sunday goers can now depart without fear
because you promised that God promised
to watch over us.

They file out, each waiting to touch your peace-giving hand.
They leave to endure seven days
until you roar, sermonize and rock
behind your holy podium,
serving His polished word.

I follow these once-a-weekers
even though I know
that beneath that black robe
it is all rehearsed.

## When August turns to October

Winter is coming.
The rain has begun, pouring herself
down over our bodies, our flowers.
It rushes down the streets, carrying with it
the last of summer,
washing the rainbow chalk off the sidewalks,
clearing the dust from the bicycle wheels,
and beating down the late flower blooms.
The rain is rushing summer out,
taking with it my daughters' cries,
the warm sunshine, the stuffy porch,
the slow turns of the fan.

## Bio: Laura P. McCarty

Laura P. McCarty was born in Ashland, Kentucky. She graduated from the University of Texas at Austin where she studied poetry with resident poet David Wevill and visiting poet Pattiann Rogers. Thanks to the kindness of Pulitzer Prize Poetry Winner Henry Taylor, Laura was able to unofficially participate in poetry workshops at American University. Laura's poetry has been published in the *GW Review* and she was a selected poet with the Trim Tab University Press Poetry Reading Series in 1993.

As a journalist, her articles have appeared in *50 Things You Can Do to Save the Planet;* *National Parks* magazine; *Nation's City Weekly; Los Angeles Times Syndicate; AAA World; Zoo World; Riverbanks*, *Language of Literature Paperback Program; Harriet Tubman!; Austin Magazine*; *West Austin News;* and the literary compilation *House of Die Drears.* Her article "Bound for Freedom" has been included on North Carolina's public library recommended reading lists for middle school.

She has lived and worked in Laos and Vietnam and has traveled extensively in Africa, Asia and Latin America. Laura and her husband Dan have five children – two of hers, three of his. They live in Arlington, Virginia, with Laura's two daughters. Both of her daughters are writers.

# MY SISTER

*Encounters*

Penny Ingle Bagby

**Wordsworth — USA, 1992**
    (a response to a poem written by Wordsworth to
    Milton entitled *London, 1802*)

As you once needed Milton, we need you.
Transport us now to England's rocky shores!
Sweet innocence and solace we pursue
Among the rainbows dancing on the moors.
The world is too much with us still at times,
A sordid realm of deadlines and demands.
We need the truth you teach us in your rhymes,
Mystical world you fashioned through your hands —
A beauteous earth with spirits bold and blithe,
Ethereal visions, solitary bowers,
Rustic folk, who work with staff and scythe,
April mornings, valleys, yews and flowers.
Wordsworth! in our dreams we seek you still —
    An Evening Star beyond the daffodil.

**Sentimental Journey**

Dazed foreigner
Standing
In my own country
At a busy checkout counter
Currency in my hand
"Here's your change, ma'am"
Embellished metal
Sporting strange faces
Stranger places
Babbling voices fill the air.

On the street
Familiar sights cleverly
Evade my eyes
No meaning in
The glare of sunshine
Sunshine on my hair.

Something deep inside me beckons
Eyelids now so tightly closed
Images appear before me
Of a home no longer there.

Damp smell of a wooden porch swing
Branches creak above my head
Fresh cut grasses form a blanket
Or a bed.

Tiny yellow wildflowers
Edge the vacant street
Mother's voice calls me
Home to eat.

**Re-vision**

Just yesterday
Brown, gray,
Charcoal, beige, ochre
Overlaid, inlaid,
Blended together
Winter colors.
Winter fields, winter trees,
Winter trunks, winter weeds
Oh, but today — !
Branches delineated
Dark against light,
Heather, umber — stark
Against the white,
Powdery drifts,
Plowed rows neatly filled,
Tree limbs cunningly striped,
— Transformation —
Rare snow in a
Texas countryside.

**Death Was Different Then**

The narrow road was dusty and mostly untraveled
And the others in the car were silent.
Efficient funeral director, attendants,
Shiny hearse, chrome casket
Had laid to rest his wife of more than sixty years.
The old man had a lot of time to think about death
As the little road from Rumley took him home.

And now he spoke calmly of events he'd never
Cared to tell, the memory was so painful still.
"Death was different then," he began,
"Lee Roy was so sick and we lived
Away out in the country.

"The old doctor did the best he could
But what he did just made it worse
So Lee Roy was near gone when we
Borrowed the neighbor's Model-T to
Take him sixty miles to the hospital.

"It was mid-December, cold and foggy
So foggy I near couldn't see the road ahead.
Beams of that old Model-T didn't cast very far.
Sometimes I even had to stop and step out
To see which way the road was going.
Course, we finally did reach the hospital
But there wasn't much could be done for him
By then and he died there the day after that.
We got a pine box from the funeral place
To put his body in.

Only 13 he was and that sad wood coffin
In the back seat all the long trip home."
He paused then for so long it seemed
He'd said all he was willing to
Of the loss of his first-born.
Then he spoke again, voice thinned with
Forty-six years of emotion and pain.
"And the burying — those days
The neighbors did the digging for you.
No one expected you to dig the grave
For your own. But afterwards" ... he sighed,

"... we covered the grave, all of us —
You didn't walk away like folks do now
With the actual putting in the ground
Done by someone else
When family and friends are gone.

"I can still hear those old hard chunks
Landing on that poor pine box.
That's the saddest sound in the world."
He rose abruptly and left the room
Trailing an aura of loneliness
And tragedy.

Death
Is always sad
Is always decisive
Is always rending
But somehow
Death
Was different then.

**Piece of Glass**

It is difficult to walk anywhere and not notice
a piece of blue or green or amber glass
lying on asphalt in a parking lot or on
a concrete curb near the park. Through
refracted sunlight it winks at me,
teasing me, urging a response.
My unwilling mind resists but my eyes
are nonetheless drawn to any simple fragment
I might spy as my childhood mind
entreats me for a critical evaluation
of a seemingly imperfect wedge
usable now only because it is broken.

I am perplexed by this fanciful
fascination – far into my sixth decade.
I have no rational use for this
rune which beckons me to pick it up.
Why has my brain insisted
for 60 years that the search
for an improvised childhood
game piece is still important?
I see the faded image of a sidewalk
and a carefully drawn chalk design.
Hour after hour we hopped,
never tiring of the game of balance,
pitching that perfect piece of glass
into just the correct space – hop,
hop, hop forward, turning, then
hop, hop, hop back to square one.

At the end of a long afternoon
of hopscotch, I would carefully
slide my piece of glass into a
pocket for safekeeping, though
not, however, honoring it as an amulet.
Because as I would wend my way home
from my friend's house I knew
I was always openly seeking
a better piece, ready to trade
this for another – one just the right
shape, one that could travel easily through
the warm air, land with determination
in the correct chalk box, and glisten
there as I approached – hop, hop, hop.

## The Question — A Villanelle

Our own sad world in pain and turmoil lies
With fears and wounds and tears enough to bear —
Why do we seek more worlds beyond our skies?

The stargazers and writers fantasize
Of distant worlds' technologies to share.
Our own sad world in pain and turmoil lies.

Old treaties fail, and countries fall and rise
And greedy plots abound, no soul to spare —
Why do we seek more worlds beyond our skies?

And some would say (in answer) they surmise
Solutions to our problems are out there.
Our own sad world in pain and turmoil lies.

Our bloodied rivers flow, and fire-filled skies
Add daily to a weighty load of care —
Why do we seek more worlds beyond our skies?

And since there is no lasting compromise,
Astronomers and scientists beware!
Our own sad world in pain and turmoil lies —
Why do we seek more worlds beyond our skies?

**The Friend**

The poet clasps my hand
with frank familiarity and,
though in the beginning we are
at arm's length, the thoughts being
shared draw me in and I am
willingly engaged in this stroll.

As we proceed down the path I
nod my head in agreement and
we incline our souls toward
each other in relationship,
as two heads nearly touching,
a mutual accord.

Frequent visitation allows
fresh insight to germinate
and essences previously too
subtle to permit possession
slip easily into my mind,
an arm now on my shoulder.

The script nears its end and I
hesitate, so my friend's hand slides
gently into my own and offers
a brief squeeze as a sweet promise,
so that I smile and close the book.

## Jackrabbits

Peering out the expansive back windows
I am mesmerized by the peace of sunset
until my mind is pricked by movement.
My eyes flick back and forth wishing to confirm
the stimulant, and yes, emerging from distant
trees and undergrowth, grasses and wildflowers,
they approach, their habit each evening in the dusk.

There are three, two of them larger and
parental, and as they advance cautiously
I smile, thinking surely we have a splendid
reputation among the meek of native
hill country animals. No dogs or cats, our
property is one of silence and safe haven
for countless local vegetarians.

Approaching the maintained portion of acreage,
they slow and move apart, finding the leafy
plants they seek among confrontational weeds that
demand space for themselves among bermuda
blades. The sun's last rays pierce the amazing
pinkness of erect ears ever on alert, extended
appendages rising far into the air.

As colors fade from the horizon I begin to
lose the outlines of their shapes and ease
back from my post at the windows, content
now to let the darkness come.

**Feather in the Wind**

From across the room a large brown
feather appears to blow back and forth
in the brisk summer wind which sweeps
across the shade of the long covered
porch, but as I approach I see the lone
squirrel who visits our live oak trees.

He is lying with finesse, stretching
out flat on his stomach, legs splayed,
bound to the cool cement, oblivious to
surroundings. The tail blows willy-nilly,
east, then west, as the squirrel naps with
aplomb, unperturbed in the August breeze.

**Insolent Insomnia**

Well into the second hour of
sleeplessness I roll onto my back
weary of rearranging a body that
seeks the physical and mental ease
necessary to fall asleep and earnestly
ponder this verb so commonly used.
Fall. Because it happens suddenly?
Unexpectedly? It is obviously
an unwilling act as no one can
force natural sleep. Fall asleep.
Who had chosen this active verb
for such a passive action? Suitors
of slumber who tonight share my
plight rue with me our inability to
participate in that elusive moment.

I allow my eyes to open and gaze up
at shadows of charcoal against gray,
the discernable motion of fan blades
against a tray ceiling. My mind
engages the familiar dark scene
accented by tiny energy thieves –
an accommodating orange glow
encircling a dimmer switch,
miniature red and green rectangles
of a surge protector, the outlines
on clocks that tell hour and minutes
but muffle the frustrating ticks.

Forcing my lids to shut tightly
I experience the peripheral flashes
of brightness that threaten retinal
misbehavior and marvel at the
plethora of physical complaints
that assault our bodies as we age.
I pepper myself with questions –
Why can others sleep but I
cannot? What is the cause of
disturbances to natural rhythm?
Is it better to rise or to hope for
peaceful resolution?

**Cottontails**

Living in the city once again with a
manicured lawn, I mourn the loss of daily
visits from larger-than-life jackrabbits.

Moving and stacking pots near the humming
compressor I jump back suddenly – reaction
to movement at my feet, long accustomed
wariness near possible snake habitat.

A crevice at the base of the concrete
slab presents three tiny heads with bodies
so meshed and interfused they appear
to be only one, sporting multiple legs and
cottontails. I blink back at them, serene
in the knowledge that the gifts of life
are everywhere, even here.

**Shhh ...**

Following cherished forms of rhyme and meter
she marks the page in childish script,
words out of sequence forced to conform
spouting four line verses with abab cdcd

Experimenting with maturing emotions
she presses words forcefully through graters
of desire, possibility, conviction, packing all
neatly into sonnets, sestinas, villanelles

Easing through life's unexpected transitions
she breathes wistful lines through sighs or moans,
with delight, solace, understanding, memory
composing themselves freely into gifts to share.

A voice speaks but she is not the subject.
She raises her eyes in expectation but she is not seen.
A hand reaches out and she awaits in uncertainty.
It rests on her pen that it not move again.

**May-lstrom**

Radiant sunlit day in May and
as I drive my mind romps, devising
metaphors and similes of landscape and
roadway traffic.  A rounded hill on which
small buildings create two eyes, a nose, and
at bottom a dark tunnel entry the maw
of a titan's head, swallowing cars and trucks,
mere pieces of sausage forced to satiate
a voracious appetite.  A freeway flyover with
cars inching forward becomes patient children
in line with inner tubes and floats waiting
a turn on the waterslide chute.  Suddenly a
concussive sound interrupts, felt keenly
in my foot on the pedal and I question
quite briefly the source.  Disorderly rubber
projectiles discharge from the back of
a diesel on all those who follow.  Two cars
react, swerve, stagger, kiss, and fragment
into a thunderhead of dust,
smoke, flame, detritus.

**Persistence**

The poem taps me on the shoulder
and I shrug it back. I am driving in
city traffic, words flowing unchecked
through my mind, twisting, dipping
like a ribbon in the wind.
Putting groceries into the pantry I
sense the poem pressing into my side
like a needy animal. Again I shrug it off –
not now I protest but words are ever
before me, crowding cans and packages.
Stirring the contents of pots on the stove
I ward off the pestering poem with a
promise of later, later. The words ride on
puffs of steam, vigorous, curling upwards,
begging me to record their expression.
On a late evening walk with my husband
I fail to follow the conversation. The poem
teases me with imaginative lines, colorful
baubles of thought bumping against my
stride, impeding my gait, my prattle.
Time to sleep but I relent, no longer
ignoring the pleading pout of the poem,
proud words insisting on recognition, their
own permanent record. In honor of
persistence, the poem lives.

## Margarita with Salt

Grains of sodium cling to the edge
of a frosted vessel, fine stemware graced
with red jalapenos and bright green leaves
adorning this transparent pale emerald
glass filled with slivers of ice
floating in redolent smooth liquid.
Pungent aroma of fresh cut lime strokes
my glands into instant reaction
filling my mind with anticipation,
my mouth with moisture as I lift the
coveted goblet, extend my tongue, lick
salty granules, and slowly swallow
the sweetly contemplated acidic margarita,
requisite rejoinder to our scintillating summer.

## The Drought

The drought
  is here
Day after day
  fruitless dust
  blows into a
  yielded expectant face,
Dehydrated hope
  that drought
  is temporary
Grit
  can be washed away
  only with tears
  of fresh felt loss,
  of broken promises,
  of unsatisfied dreams
The drought arrived
  as predicted
  and persists with its
  built-in prohibitions
Seek precious liquid memories —
  store them, hide them,
  against the day
  the drought
  consumes your soul.

**Escape Plan**

Spring's fresh colors
Sprinkled confetti
Double rainbow set above
Vibrant redbud
Calling
Look at me.
Let's go bounding
Through the fields
Lie down and
Face the skies,
Find no ugly
Surprise
Like a spider
Or snakes
Only a soft pallet
On which to sigh,
A cheerful sparrow
Brushing the sky
A curious squirrel
Twitching his eye.

## Fog

Evening ...
    Masses of drifting fog descend on saturated treetops
    Shrouds of mist obscure and blur impressions
    Accents vanish in the turbid haze
    Fading yellow orbs of blushing light
    Mystical eerie spheres, scattered beacons
    Landmark stains bruise the darkening sky
Clouds in spiritual union with the earth.

**Second Verse**

A
Sudden
Feeling of
Omniscience
Surges over me
Like the giant breakers
At the beach and
Retreats as
Quickly.

## The Butter Knows

All week long the butter
sitting in its reserved spot on the counter
in a lovely covered candy dish
has puddled slightly around the edges
of its rectangular prism
as temperatures outside grew.
Even though the air conditioner ran
and the house was a cool container,
the butter knew that outside
people still wore tank tops and shorts,
so the oil of the butter crept and
lightly outlined the fatty yellow cream.
Each butter pat spread easily and quickly,
melting like a lover as soon as it touched
the warmth of biscuit or roll.
And then the norther blew in, having
lost none of its fury as it
visited states northwest of us
on its way from the icebound Arctic,
and the temperatures descended so
suddenly that, though we had been warned,
citizens complained boisterously
about the depths of the bitter plunge.
The central heating hums
throughout the house, assuring
everyone of comfort.
The fresh butter stick sits primly
and fastidiously in the crystal,
not at all surprised,
solid and sure.

## Recess in Tynan

Drought —
first half of the decade,
the 50's, the girls gathered on
the large dusty playground
of our South Texas school.

Fallen branches
from the few trees
made excellent brooms.
Daily we swept the ground clean,
filled our hands with
small white rocks,
outlined our dream houses.
Unaware of floor plans,
we delineated bedrooms,
a bathroom, a kitchen,
a living room,
allowed for requisite doorways,
afterward hosting one another
as guests
touring our future homes.

Then we dusted our hands,
joined a line for the jump rope –
an inch thick, substantial,
at least twelve feet long,
a teacher at one end, a child at the other.
Chanting the familiar themes
we jumped in and our feet pounded
the well-packed dirt as
"twenty four robbers
came a-knocking at the door."

**Endowment**

The pen is held by her hand
and as she spreads her thoughts
on paper the ink begins to flow
more evenly and entreaties press
with confidence onto the surface
and stain the receiving element

introspections keening, mourning
contemplations lauding, stroking
revelations shocking, grieving
meditations praising, seeking

Observations and perceptions
become living missives to those who
mature in her quixotic shade as
pens slide into the hands of primed and
eager young with messages of their own

deliberations probing, striking
propositions vexing, clashing
objections kindling, coping

Aging essence of her mind betrays as
gleanings of endeavors display
ragged and uneven, the script now
less fruitful, halting, diminished
scrawling across the page

Irrevocably the pen ceases to register
visions imprint invisible creases
declarations no longer ink, but spirit.

## A Tie That Binds

Your voice
Trembles
As you
Reach out
Across the miles
Across the months
It's been so long
Since we last spoke
And infinite days since
We were last together.

Your weariness
Disappointment
Hurt and crying need
For closeness to be
Reality
Compel me to
Reach inside
Myself and find
Some lost connection.

I've felt your
Stirring thoughts before
You know
And that is why
You seek me now
That wave length
We have always shared
Though buried
Still is there.
And as we grope

And you begin
To speak your fears
Those deep
Throbbing pulses
Beat out and
Communion
Is complete.

I replace the receiver
Your voice
Gone
Tenuous union
Severed
Tightened throat
Tear dampened eyes
Turn back to an
Immediate demanding
World yet

Insistent
Strident
Ringing
Your voice crawls
Through my mind
I feel you're here
Beside me and perhaps
You feel me now
Within your walls
Sharing a burden
That overwhelmed you
Not so very many
Moments
Ago.

**Facsimile**

Through paired curtains teased
  by a summer breeze
  moving almost imperceptibly
  through the dimness
I watch the boys playing,
  contorting and twisting
  young bodies in impossible
  shapes on cool grass
Sky so gray, so almost-not-there,
  not the shocking sunset
  of moments ago,
  nor a royal parade ground for stars –
  just a frustrating, dusky nothingness
Somehow a frightening reflection
  of myself.

**Chalk Story**

Joyful songs reverberate
In the night air and then
A hushed expectancy fills the
Open air Tabernacle as
A lone figure rises and
Stands at the crude altar
With blank paper
And colored chalks.
Her clear resonant voice
Begins to tell an old story
And grasses and rocks
The sun and strange-clothed
Peoples take their places
As her hands trace a path
Into days long gone by.
Quite suddenly I realize
I'm walking somewhere
In the past
Down a dusty trail
Searching for the timeless
Truths I know are there.
And as I bow my head,
Tears streaming down,
Strong hands reach out to me
Compassionate arms enfold me
And looking up
I know I've met
The Master face to face.

**Dispossessed**

Midnight in the hill country,
I watched the large block
Of unfettered moonlight that
Shifted across the tile floor
As the moon crawled
Across the southern sky
Past our many windows.

The glass prisms in the door
That led to the garden
Made fanciful designs on
Furniture and walls
Out of the shining, smiling,
Radiant, bold whiteness that
Playfully entreated me.

That pale yellow moon
Spread its benevolence
Over our land, our house, our bodies
And customary sleep
Would have denied the visitation,
A gift of the symphonic
Nocturne of splendor.

But we live in the city now.

My eyes question the sheers on
The windows, unable to distinguish
Moonlight amidst all the other lights —
Street lights, porch lights, headlights,
So much incandescence and fluorescence,
Such frustrating interference —
Oh, for extreme moonlight!

**Image**

Thirty-four years stare back
At me
From the mirror and yet
Deep within this
Frame
Lurks
A young girl,
Dreamer
Who still
Expects to play
Rachmaninoff
With three encores
To become
A famous
Broadway actress
To sing at
The Met
Someday
Dreamer
Of exotic
Places
Richly garbed
With trees
And skies
Still in
My
Eyes.

**To My Mother (Mother's Day, 1979)**

Beginning
As a bud tight folded
Secretive
Even the hue unknown
Then slowly, patiently
Developing
Revealing smooth petals
Each a special
Nuance
Gently blooming
Into innocent array
And even now
Time changes you
Into subtly
Variegated
Soft velvet
Surprising even those
Who know you best
With pleasing angles
And furls
Unnoticed till now
Delicate blooming beauty
Seeming replete
And yet
Deep in the center
Of your substance
The core
Tight covered
Still.

**Forgiving Child**

Morning,
And you stall
As usual
Playing in the breakfast
Cereal
And the clock shows
I will be late
Again.
Yelling, pushing,
Threatening, forcing,
You must hurry or
I will be late
Again.
Tears and cereal
Are choked down
Sobbingly
While I tower
Over you.
Then quick brush
Your hair
Get
In the car
Race
The motor
Hurry you off
To school
And as you step
From the car
You turn
Smiling and
Blow me a kiss
As usual.

## Petition — A Villanelle

Our love has come unraveled at the seams,
Harsh words are always hanging in the air,
And where are all my childhood hopes and dreams?

And finding that we play on separate teams,
Confusion mocks me even in my prayer.
Our love has come unraveled at the seams.

Once love enveloped us like soft moonbeams,
But now a cherished moment is so rare.
And where are all my childhood hopes and dreams?

Futility and rage are our extremes,
How hard it is for us to mend the tear!
Our love has come unraveled at the seams.

Then creeping from the past the vision gleams
— You were a knight and I a maiden fair —
And where are all my childhood hopes and dreams?

We must go once again to love's warm streams —
I hear there is a healing fountain there.
Our love has come unraveled at the seams,
And where are all my childhood hopes and dreams?

## Ah, Tchaikovsky!

Come on, sweet music, wrap me in your folds,
And stroke my ragged psyche with your note
Till all the fear and pain the day now holds
Are neutralized by your pure antidote.
Imprint your pristine outline in my mind,
Dispel the shameless doubts that skulk inside,
Then coax the cord that binds me to unwind
And rinse away the caustic tears of pride.
Just take me, vanished artist, grip me tight —
You must not lose me now we've come so far —
And show me all the dreams you dreamed each night
Whose shattered forms became a falling star,
And I will whisper how your agony
Is daily now an ecstasy to me.

**White Beauty**

Ice Storm!
  And morning reveals
      White trees prostrate
          burdened with new radiance
      Regally adorned
          in glistening brilliance
      Garments overspread
          with flashing glitter
      Fresh-cut gems
          alight with dawn's first splendor
      Crystalline enlaced
          on beaming branches
      Royal jewels displayed
          in pomp and glory
      A myriad
          of fragile sparkling diamonds
      Winter's Coronation.

**Conflict!**

    Reproachful looks, chilling accusations
    Faults recounted, charges, piercing scorn
    Rebound of emotion, cutting, rending
    Broken spirits sever love's thin bindings
    Discord in the night when wounds are opened
    Verdicts sound, sacred vows lay broken.

## A Soldier's Peace

I watch the hostile skies that threaten gloom
As slanting fires derange an austere land.
A quickened sand dune sighs a languid plume
And missile's lyres produce a liquid sand.
The carcass of a mutilated tank
Is whistling low its shrill and trembling breath.
I scan the pale horizon from a bank
Where gritty blasts deliver wounds or death.
The blistered region cleanses blackened walls,
Reshapes abraded tracts with countless grains.
Amid demolished ruins a scorpion crawls
And pierces with his tail the pungent stains.
I seek among the hills where blood was shed
An inner peace when outer peace has fled.

*1991*

**The Praying of the Creed**

Organ music softly hums bare whispers
    through the spacious sanctuary.


How strange it all appears
    and foreign.
Ah, Father, how far I have traveled,
    how long I have tarried
Before coming again to a place where
    I seek Your face.
The worship begins and I join in
    feeling my way as one with restored sight
Not yet used to moving without reaching,
    touching.
All stand to recite the creed and I grasp
    the printed bulletin

How did I come to be here at this moment?

Three lively women knocking at my door: Oh, come and feel and share with us – "Evangelism Explosion" they said and I had hesitated (You know, Father, how long, how many years), but after all I had a child now two years old and so I said OK, this Sunday, I will come

I turn to the "Apostles Creed" and begin to read the words

*I believe in God the Father Almighty, maker of heaven and earth*

And crashing down upon me His awesome presence becomes so real, the paper trembles in my hand, darts invade my eyes.

***"Be still and know that I am God"***

*and in Jesus Christ his only son our Lord*

My mind races back, back, and I'm a child again in Sunday School, His picture hanging on the wall and He is knocking, knocking at a door

**"hear my voice and open the door"**

*who was conceived by the Holy Spirit*

I watch as an angel speaks the promise to a young maiden

**"For with God nothing shall be impossible"**

*born of the Virgin Mary*

The crudely made manger in our Christmas play — but how real it all seemed, how joyous as we celebrated the birth of the Christ child

**"born this day in the city of David, a Saviour, which is Christ the Lord"**

*suffered under Pontius Pilate*

The scene changes dramatically and I stand afar off while my Saviour faces alone the whip, the spittle, the humiliation in the night

**"And they spit upon him, and took the reed, and smote him"**

*was crucified*

I am devastated again with Peter ("Be it far from thee, Lord!" I cry) and stretched between two thieves beneath the sky He moans. I am torn in wretchedness, eyes now too full to hold the tears, a stone caught in my throat "crucified him ... and sitting down they watched him there"

*dead*

Throbbing pulses in my soul beat out, beat out till thunderous in my heart they strive to tear me from the pew I clutch so fiercely

"Father into thy hands"

*and buried*

Pictures flashing, a rock in front of the tomb, soldiers guarding

"they went and made the sepulchre sure, sealing the stone, and setting a watch"

*The third day he rose from the dead*

The stone rolled away, an angel telling the seekers that they look for Him there in vain

"Why seek ye the living among the dead? He is not here but is risen"

*He ascended into heaven*

A hillside — was the day sunny and cloudless, the blue reading from horizon to horizon with the sea stretched out below? Or was it gray and windy as those disciples watched Him ascending, peering long after Him into the rolling murky clouds

"while he blessed them, he was parted from them, and carried up into heaven"

*and sitteth at the right hand of God the Father Almighty;
from thence he shall come to judge the quick and the dead*

And as Stephen saw Him, I see Him in his majesty, glory, honor

**"those things which are above, where Christ sitteth on the right hand of God"**

*I believe in the Holy Spirit*

Sweet Holy Spirit, how I have grieved You, but still You seek the prodigal, whispering "Return" — tranquility touches my bruised but eager soul

**"Quench not the Spirit"**

*the holy catholic church*

Oneness with all the Christians of the world overwhelms and startles me — people, people all over the world today worshiping God the Father, Christ Jesus, Holy Spirit — one flesh, one body

**"by one Spirit are we all baptized into one body"**

*the communion of saints*

A fresh white cloth, small bits of bread, tiny glasses filled with shimmering purple, prayers and penitence, peace and permanence

**"in remembrance of me"**

*the forgiveness of sins*

My life looms black before me, sure, all those small ones, Lord, but what of those big ones, the ones You know about, the ones I dare not even think about, those SINS with capitals, dear Father, bless Your holy name, for You forgive even those

**"as far as the east is from the west"**

*the resurrection of the body and the life everlasting. Amen.*

Tears, tears, flowing so profusely now, but God shall wipe away every tear, and death will be no more and He will give me a new heart, a new heaven, a new earth, world without end.

**"Even so, come, Lord Jesus"**

## New Beginnings — A Villanelle

The fields are full, with harvest on the way.
The first cool breath of fall is in the air.
Death brings a new beginning, so they say.

The night is stealing moments from the day.
The kitchen table shields an empty chair.
The fields are full, with harvest on the way.

Green summer leaves perform a quaint ballet
But soon the limbs and branches will be bare.
Death brings a new beginning, so they say.

So quietly a life is stripped away —
The world whirls on as if it doesn't care.
The fields are full, with harvest on the way.

And what of those who've been assigned to stay,
With no one left to comfort and to share?
Death brings a new beginning, so they say.

Dear Father, help the ones who strive to pray
For strength and hope that seem no longer there.
The fields are full, with harvest on the way.
Death brings a new beginning, so they say.

**Personalities in Wood**

A haughty defiant
Giant
With gaunt, gnarled limbs
Twisted, grasping branches
Swords to battle the
Icy, blistering wind
Ageless body
Disfigured with
Scars of former years

A prim unruffled
Countess
Dignity undisturbed by
Nature's violence
Bare branches lifted
In perfect symmetry
Indifferent to a frozen
Broken
Landscape

A gentle drooping
Maiden
Disrobed
Stripped of modesty,
Crying for the majesty
Of summer leaves
Weeping for the
Virgin vestments,
Writhing, trembling
              in the throes of winter's storm.

**Kaleidoscope**

Forest trees with interwoven color

> lemon drenched with scarlet slashes,
> orange velvet-vested and purple peppered,
> rust-dusted and crimson spattered

One tree multi-colored, a giant butterfly asleep
> in the wooded pine finery

Warm colors fan out from the depths of another
> kaleidoscope fashion

Flags of miniature red leaves on towering twins
> salute a coral solo

Beyond, mere whispers of leaves antique gold
> and bare twigs crocheted in lacy patterns

Over the road, branches of rounded leaves
> now copper coins dangling, jangling,
> jingling, clinking in the gusting wind

All in startling contrast to the evergreen pompoms
> of the pines.

**Palette**

Rare autumn currency
Richly prized hematite
Gilded beryl
Hues of citrine
Metamorphic leaves on hardwoods
Cushioned
By the pines

Ornate treasure
Minted ocher
Transient semi-precious ores
Opulent topaz
Meteoric corundum
In changing luster
Now bountiful

Coveted currency
Hoarded fortune
Too soon buried.

**Mood Music**

Winter's song
        a brief pastoral symphony

Lustrous instruments
        garnished white play flats and sharps
        in minor key

Frigid gusts
        of wind vibrate quaint tinkling
        cymbals

Slender fingers
        of ice on lofty xylophones perform
        a soft sonata

Bittersweet melodies
        waft from tiny rhythmic bells on
        brittle boughs

Shimmering
        crystal wind chimes create a
        natural harmony

Melancholy
        muted notes of consonance

Mood music
        composed in winter solstice.

**Esperanza**

Waving jubilant greetings
brightly in the August heat,
long supple stems of frilly leaves
extend to observers yellow blossoms
whose mouths are open with joy.
Even here alongside the interstate exit where
I sit at a stoplight the nimble leaf-laden
boughs are thickly blessed with exuberant
displays that generate hope.  Splendid fragile
vitalities replete with generous beauty, the
blooms ride the rising breeze trumpeting
"summer, summer, summer"
and blowing me kisses.

**The Wedding Jewels**

Give to each other today
Emeralds of understanding
Intertwined with the
Dark red rubies of your dreams,
Opals of patience created
By seasons of adversity
And glistening pearls of faith
Overlaid with strength,
And then to brighten all
The days and nights
Of your life together,
The diamond of desire,
Because they say
A diamond is
Forever.

**Residue**

I pause
In wonder
Why is she singing
At this late hour
Perched high above me in
Black silhouettes
Spread out against
The darkened sky
And then I smile
And enter into praise
With the cardinal,
Nighttime caroler —
    In the third heaven
    You who made me
    Hear my voice
    How I love you
    Honor and glory
    To your name
    You who made
    Midnight mystery
    Springtime fantasy
    Moonlight magic
    Whisper softly
    Let me hear You, too.

**Exposed**

Luscious trees
Not those trees in autumn's golden hues arrayed
Nor trees on whom spring's greenery is proud displayed
Nor those with drooping branches filled with leaves for shade

No ...
I love you, trees, now stripped and bare so I can see
Your every angle, line and curve intimately —
Surveyed and measured, mentally caressed by me.

Dear trees ...
Too soon the spring will fill you with new mystery
And strength will rise, your boughs unfurl in jubilee,
Your gracious form found only in my memory.

**Oaken**

You are to me much like a winter tree
      I know your every knot and branch and limb
Your barest moments are a part of me
      I understand your impulse and your whim

Your roots are bonded deeply to the earth
      Your trunk is firmly fixed, implanted there
Rings of resolution built since birth —
      Endurance cultivated by despair

I've seen the cold wind strip you of your pride
      Adversity remove your glorious leaves
Your crusty bark protects your moist inside
      As icy weight deprives and then bereaves

You stagger at each burden, then you bend
      External cover solid and severe
A quiet seeping binds a breach, to mend
      The sighing tree emits a golden tear

And when the bleakest season passes by
      From deep within you draw forth strength and life
Renewal issues green against the sky
      And overcomes all passing pain and strife.

**Transplanted**

God reached down and
with His powerful fingers
He began to loosen
my tangled roots
from the stony soil
surrounding them
and as He tugged,
I resisted, gasping, but
the firm unyielding
grip tightened and the
vigorous drawing out
of my being by His
concentrated force
continued
until
suddenly the whole
of me dangled over
my world and I
found myself unable
to breathe, viewing
with bewilderment
a little known latitude
as He gathered all
my exposed strands
into a ball and
inserted me into
a prepared new home
of clay and sandy loam.

**Requiem for Discovery**

Mighty traveler,
dependable transport,
she leaves ethereal realms
above Canaveral
traveling north
to abide in
a sepulchre of history.
In former days, her proud prow
split the atmosphere with
scintillating urgency
and sent her to perch
on the edge of the cosmos.
Majestic, dignified,
grim visage staring
at a different kind of unknown,
destined for interment
in churlish bonds
she rides upon a cavernous carriage.
How is she not
somehow
placed in a pasture suitable
for old shuttles,
a retreat, a retirement,
worthy of her accomplishments?
Descending,
she does her victory lap
past our cold marble memorials
in Washington —
Fitting, perhaps, as her
sudden violent ascensions
have ceased,
and she, too,
will be a cold monument.

**Spring Cleaning**

Delicate white flowers
Dogwood unfolding everywhere
Heady scent of spring
Hold back! Don't violate
My mind! "Retreat!"
A command rings out but
The retreat is disorganized
Causing me to stumble
        back
            through a
                swinging door
            into
          my
        secret
    closet
Dark, dark
Musty cobwebs everywhere
Flailing arms
Touch a forbidden
Knot
In the wood and open my
Pandora's box
Anguish rushes
Into the room, lust, lies,
Hatred, greed, impatience,
Unfaithfulness
Howl through the darkness
Brush my face
Hideous sights, evil whispers crawl
About my skull
In confusion
I knock from a shelf boxes

Impurities, inconsistencies
Stored
(Out of sight, out of mind)
Where nobody
Could see
Lightheaded
Ringing in my ears
Drowns
Accusing voices
Spots
Before my eyes
Signal that
      sweet
            unconsciousness
                      takes
                              over

Snow swirling through the air
Swishing, whispering,
No, not snow,
Beautiful white buds of
Dogwood trees in the breeze
Above my head
Leaves rustling
Intimately
Urging me
Back
Salt tears wash tarnish and
Lingering pain away
Sweet fragrances
Anoint me
As I pray.

## Interview with Discovery

"I'm here to get your thoughts —
where would you like to begin?"
'You know I was part of quite a long
confinement before birth'
"Really."
'Yes, it began in the summer of 1979
but I was actually delivered in 1983'
"Well, that is long."
'We are, you see, quite complicated beings,
unlike simple rockets or your everyday jets'
"Oh, I'm sure."
She cleared her throat.
'Because of the vertical take-offs and
the horizontal landings, of course'
"Yes, of course."
'You appear to be young — perhaps you don't
remember a lot of shuttle history ...'
She became very quiet, then a near whisper:
'You know, I did lose some of my siblings'
Shaking off her momentary somber note,
she suddenly winked at a large display nearby
and changed the subject.
'That chart shows all the
many emblems — they called them
mission insignias — used for my flights —
each flight had a special design —
I couldn't say which one I liked best.'
"They are stunning pieces, certainly."
'I was always proud to do my duty —
I flew so many missions —
It was thrilling when we launched
the Hubble Space Telescope, and
then, later, serviced it as required.'

"That does sound exciting."
'I'm actually only 28, but I guess
that's like dog years or horse years
and in human years I am likely around 70 —
I suppose they think of me as old and
outdated, retired now, but I still have
a lot of miles left in me'
"You look really good."
'I understand I am to get a face lift soon so that
I will project a better appearance for my public'
She sighed.
"How do you envision your retirement — I mean,
What do you desire most in the future?"
'I think of that lovely blue marble earth
floating on a backdrop of eternity, and now ...
I just hope to be able to see a patch of sky each day'
"I'm sure my readers will find
your point of view most interesting.
Thank you so much for your time."

**Vernal Exhibitionists**

Twiggy branches of redbud trees
tightly overlaid with red-violet shreds
announce the season of spring,
spreading like blessings above
laughing Texas mountain laurels
fashionably full and green,
weighted with pendulous
purple blossoms miming
bunches of grapes.
The laurels distill a fragrance
that insists I heed and appreciate
their transitory performance
during this afternoon stroll
and I hear there are already bluebonnets
on the roadsides in the hill country.

**Vanity of Vanities**

Thumbing through colorful pages
in the slick brochure, fascinated
with the photos, I am prodded by
something internal — a primordial
instinct, an urge to rub my finger
in those powdery substances that are
coaxing, enticing, seducing me.
Images of freshly mined
earthy minerals displayed in
multiple tints of sensual color
"lotus" ... "truffle" ... "lava"
evoke covetousness and ardor.
These abundant textures of
bronze, blush, pearl, pewter, with
sheen, shimmer, satin, or matte
in nuances to caress me
with the consistency of cocoa
or confectioners' sugar,
are presented to me, the female,
as infinitely desirable
to spread upon
my face, above my eyes, or
as a soft kiss upon my cheeks.
Longing to embrace,
experience, experiment with
these velvet pigments,
I am tethered by subliminal
visceral bonds
in the marrow of my spirit, to
primeval women, ancestral ladies,
who bent to the light
to adorn themselves.

## Lunar Ritual

When we lived in
the hill country
in silent compact
we believed
we owned the moon.
Stretching our legs out
in front of the glider
we awaited its arrival
on the long, deep front porch,
serenaded in singing darkness,
scanning the horizon
and thrilling when
the glowing rambler reared
joyously to greet us.

We could watch
mesmerized,
captivated, through
unfolding hours,
rocking back and forth,
the smiling synergist
making its slow transit
through the southern sky,
startlingly bright
almost too bright
hurt-your-eyes bright
if engaged for too long.
As it curved overhead,
forced to share
our framed picture
with the lazy

**The Doves**

In the evening,
facing each other,
they ride intertwined
on a blade
of the porch fan —
I think they are
demonstrating necking,
each head rubbing up
against the neck of the other.

In early morning,
side by side on top
of the wooden fence
outside our dining room window,
they coo — I think they
are sharing lyrics — maybe
they are singing, "we've got
the sun in the morning,
and the moon at night."

outstretched limbs
of the live oaks,
we would sigh,
retreat inside,
solemnly promising
to be there again
tomorrow night,
embracing our moon.

**Lament**

My heart contracts as I turn the corner
onto Sunrise Road, passing senior apartments
where Mom lived so many years. I am awash
in messages from my senses. I hear
her voice as she opens the door and the
less familiar voice of someone reading
a book of scientific or historical
significance or a novel, tapes sent
by the state – books for the blind.

I see her as she hurries to turn it off,
smiling at me, and I feel her thin shoulders
and grasp her firm hands as we cling to
each other briefly. I wonder what part
of me she sees through eyes so deeply
affected by disease. I embrace her laughter
as I relate something clever about one
of her many great grandchildren.

I smell the unmistakable scent
of the goat milk body wash she always
uses, breathe deeply of the contents of
her bookcases — disintegrating textbooks
used for teaching English or paperbacks
for Great Books discussions at the downtown
library. I give a mental nod to a friendly and
comforting perfume she wore for decades.

It is so difficult to force myself to drive on.
I long to be able to put time in reverse, to
stop the car, to hurry in, to enfold her,
give her my attention, my time,
my love.     But     she's     gone.

**Sweeping Up Shards**

Rhythmically sweeping fine shards
of words and phrases which converge into
a pile filled with fractured feelings
as fine and clear, as sharp and edgy,
as truth itself, I construct a detailed whole
forming without permission in my mind …

Reaching cautiously to arrange and re-arrange
small units of expression that can mend
the outer margins of splintered meaning,
I smooth exhortation with revelation,
soothe prophecy with promise,
and fresh reality surges onto the page.

**Family Anthology**

Deftly choosing first this one,
Then that —
Riffling through
A stack of papers
Valuable perhaps
In our eyes only —
Surveying again the written lines:
So many questions
Some answered
Others not
A few riddles
For which there may be
No answers
Lilting charmers
Lift me up
Then
The breathless meeting
With a firebrand
Searing, seething
Hurrying past
That far too dangerous
Stiletto
I haven't fully
Confronted as yet.
Your poems are you
And still they're so much more —
Intimate constant friends
I summon at will —
Gifts of yourselves
Ordered with daring and skill.

**Brief Sojourn**

I hold the poem like a friend holds my hand
and immerse myself in its substance
as one would sink down into a warm bath
filled with comforting scents in healing oils that
offer satisfying liquid caresses.
I breathe deeply as the lines of familiar words
rush into my mind offering relief and consolation,
leading me down a path of contentment
lined with pleasing pebbles of the past.

**Writing Poetry**

Forming
words into phrases
selecting
rejecting
replacing
hesitating
Precisely
ordering
my thoughts
rearranging
changing
framing
Turning words
over
in my mind
looking at their edges
like an expectant
puzzler
wanting the
guaranteed
accurate
outcome –
Oh!
the pieces
won't
fit so
put them away
try another day

**Creating**

I wrote a lot of poetry
at the park yesterday
in my head
I folded my thoughts carefully
into fragile
Paper airplanes
And sent them winging
through the skies to find
A resting place
So many perfect lines
floating on sweet
Summer scented air
Guided in sunlight
and dappled shadow
by the Spirit
Who created them
Guiltless offerings —
I could not keep them
For myself —
They were His.

## Bio: Penny Faith Ingle Bagby

Penny Faith Ingle Bagby was born in Corpus Christi, Texas. After completing a year of college, she and her husband Tom transferred to Delta State College in Mississippi where he graduated and she attended college part-time and worked for the university. Upon returning to Texas his job moved them about and she attended several other universities, graduating finally from East Texas Baptist College with a Bachelor of Arts degree. She did post-graduate work at Mary Hardin-Baylor.

Penny won the Era Miller Award for creative writing at East Texas Baptist College. She was published in the college literary book, The Beacon. She was also honored with several awards from the Mockingbird Poetry Society, a branch of The Poetry Society of Texas.

As a teacher of primary grades in many Texas towns, Penny encouraged her students to read and write poetry. The students were given a collection of poems for choral reading which included an introduction to authors they might study in high school. During the years she worked in Celina, she helped students enter their poetry in a yearly area contest.

Penny and her husband Tom reside in Round Rock, Texas. They have three sons – the eldest is a coach and teacher; one twin is a builder and the other is a financial advisor. Ten grandchildren keep them very busy attending school performances and athletic competitions.

Penny continues to produce new poetry.

# MY SELF

*Murmurs*

*Patricia Ruth*

## Forest Oasis

Breaking through the earth's crust
With a sharp jolt,
Greeting the air
The seed bursts
Giving life to the first leaf
Reaching for the sunlight's warmth,
Straining upward.
The soil parts, rocks tumble aside
In this isolated place.
All the fragments of this world
Recognize this life force,
Insistent on its spreading.
Taking hold, forcing roots stubbornly down,
God's newest miracle expands.
Watch this thin branch growing eagerly
Into giant size in this sheltered grove.
Do you believe the seed still contains the power
To survive all the dangers that could wither it?
There is no one but you observing the magic
Understanding too well that all that lives is fragile.
Dream with me of spring bringing
Exotic, elegant flowers hanging heavy
On thick, woody stems.

**Song of a Kentucky Visit**

I'm taken by surprise by this visit.
It's the trees that did it.
A magic transportation into another time.
Suddenly, I'm a young woman again,
Sitting on my porch,
Two babies on my knees,
The rest not born, nor thought of.
I'm singing some off-key tune
No Kentucky melody with a lute,
Just a song of my own making.
Tiny heads rest against my breast,
As we listen to the soft sounds
Of Autumn in the hollers.
All along the ridges,
The trees —
Gilded orange,
Amber glow,
Burning crimson,
Spread against the darkened sky.
Like hands held out
In one last,
Futile plea
Trying to stall off winter.
I refocus my eyes —
My gaze is fixed on New York trees.
I'm returned from my wanderings.
I always knew I'd go back,
I just didn't know when,
Or how,
Or that it would be
From this place,

And for so short a stay,
But I'm glad it was
Autumn
In the hollers.

## The Day in the Navy Dress

It was so hot, in my navy dress,
As we strolled down the street
In fall sunshine.
Our bodies were so close,
Nearly pressing as we walked,
Side by side,
Laughing,
Remembering,
The exchange of knowing smiles.

If I just could have spoken,
Reached out with words,
My God, do not let me leave,
Hold me,
Stop me.

If you could have pressed
My head to your chest,
Fingers clasped within my hair,
I could have sobbed my fears.

But no
We stood there,
Three feet apart,
Crooking little fingers,
A cool good-bye,
Dozens of promises,
About next time,
Spanning the chasm.

Turning,
You walked up the stairs

I walked the other way.

But that is not the end
My mind
Will let me leave.

Instead I've ceased all motion,
Paralyzed time,
The setting is the street,
The sun is hot,
And I'm in my navy dress.

**Mirage**

The ghost of your face
Flickered briefly
In the mirror of my mind.
Doubled now, then single,
Drifting away
Shadows losing depth.
If I could only hold it longer
But with morning it escapes,
Defying my desire.
No pastel images
Can keep their shape
In light so bright.
Closing on the vision
It has disappeared.

**Far Sojourner**

Gliding, bending
Over the red-topped trees
Is a lonely reed bird.

She moves to the tune
Of chilled air
Tearing at barren ground.

This forgotten one,
Alone, drifts
Under a misted sun.

She looses her reminiscent melody
As she spins by
A scraggly mesquite,

Only visitor
Touring
Our wintered land.

**Turning Aside**

I turned aside when I saw the gate,
Pausing, standing mute,
Then I slipped inside
To wander down a path forbidden,
Living dreams I never knew existed,
Bequeathing innocence to its own fate.
The path grew twisted, untreadable,
I stumbled back to where
I find the road forgotten.
Now alone, no ghost of myself,
I awake from my trance
To assume so late
The stricken guilt
Which lying idle
So ably multiplied.

## Lament from a Fig Tree

My head is blackened and bent
My arms are withered and shrunken,
My limbs are burned and dried,
I change to dust at the touch of the wind.
I, briefly lighted by the sensation of
Lightning down my length,
Stand cursed by the Master
Never to bear fruit.

**Cleo's Snake**

And what would happen
If I were to suddenly appear
Curled legs, leaning shoulders,
Mouth whispering, "I love you"?

Would you start up as if
I had been Cleo's snake?
Would you shudder and perspire,
Panic, jump and run?

Never must I speak those forbidden words
That might hang in the dark
Dropping as some great gate
Clanking down

Separating now
From tomorrow
A tomorrow to come no more.

For I would do
The unforgiveable,
Break the contract,
Nullify the agreement.

I must forever stay here,
And you stay there,
Between us miles of phone lines,

Taxis,
Trains,
Planes

I must be silent and not speak
Of anything my heart might say,
There should be only stolen hours,
Then stillness, quiet silent void

Mouths should be for kissing only,
Whispers cannot be heard,
Love must stay outside,
Never step inside passion's hour.

## Showtime

In the early morning I sit
And stare down
At my collection of jars
Checking my selection of faces.
Shall I wear the slit skirt
To become a vamp,
Or wrap my hips with sashes?
Should I pad my shoulders
And parade as office empress?
Why are you surprised to find
So many disguises
Behind my eyes?
You do not understand me.
It's only that you
Are today's audience
For the gray light choice
Of my charade.

**Moving On**

When I have swept out
The last of the dust,
Packed that remaining box,
Given away the final potted plant,
Locked the door —
If I turned quickly enough
To peer through the window,
Could I see ghosts
Still within the room?
If I planned to stay behind,
Silent in some closet
Breathing very softly,
Could I hear voices
Speaking their magic words,
Locked for eternity
In a certain time?
If I tiptoe from room to room,
Will children be babies
And you and I lovers —
In a midnight room?
If I could come back
In a quarter century,
Late some winter evening,
Would there be you and I,
Young and lean and loving,
Unchanged and fixed,
Together
Caught in the past,
Untouched by the future?

## Porter for My Dreams

I am sure you took with you
All the important things in this place,
Books, papers, records,
In a zippered clutch.
All sorts of big men's big deals,
And all your clothing pressed neatly
In bags with special hangers
That leave no crease.
Well heeled, brisk, so sure,
You sped to the airport
In just the right casual gear.

As you reached the plane's stairs,
The shiny metal slipping down your hand,
You stop —
And shake your shoulders,
Something is nagging at your mind.
You have included extra baggage
You did not want to carry.

Over your shoulder you can almost see
My persistent smile,
And hear my easy drawl.
You remember
You have the one thing
You would have left behind
My love and caring.
The feelings you do not need.

I am this peculiar substance,
Open, utterly vulnerable,
Never cured and never taught,

But also not loving often,
So I treat it gently when it comes,
Giving it room, recognizing it,
Knowing this softens me about the edges.
Your words cannot change me.

Listen —
The plane's engines are beginning.
Now, leave unfettered, go free!
Do not feel yourself to be
The porter for my dreams.
I have learned only one thing well —
Myself.
I must be this.
Now shrug your shoulders
And enter the plane.
You can travel unencumbered
Shifting a lighter load.

**Drought**

She moves among the pots
With her garden hose,
Water drips reflecting rainbows
In the heated rays
Piercing the garden shop.

The land is still
The air is stale
Birds are gone,
Frogs are gone
The monarchs skirt
This desolate space.

The crunchy remnants of grass,
Not turned to dust,
Dead trees and shrubs,
Threaten with our fear
Of fire.

Catfish Hollow, watery grave
Of a nine year old just two years past,
Now lies only
Rocky ledge
And bitter plain.

Calendars are turned again
As cloudless skies follow cloudless skies —
Sunsets devoid of color
No hint of rain to soothe
Our parched, scorched,
And withered frames.

**Grabbing the Ring**

Come with me
To ride the merry-go-round
Up and down, round and round.
Maybe we'll get
A horse that's brown
Or maybe it will be a speckled bay,
Isn't it fun to live this way?
Join in my child's dream.
This time sing with me
A song of a happy day.
Whistle me a tune I knew long ago.
Let's go back
To that playground
We loved
And a merry-go-round
On which dreams were found.

## Life's Bookkeeping

Long ago Life added the parts of Sorrow,
Protested the quick division of Love,
Revealed the sly subtraction of Time,
Deplored the faulty multiplication of Truth,
Totaled the values
And entered the small remainder.

## Prayer at Seventeen

Fill me with joy
So I know
I am not a work
Without a wit.
Fill me with pain
So I know
I am not a mass filling a void.
Giver of Life, give to me
Of both your depths.
Press upon me
The whole of you.

*1959*

## Daughter Mine

This child pushes against me
As she did against ribs, hips
Moving outward
She thrusts at me
New thoughts, views

Slowly she turns my world
On its axis
Lending me a different angle
Thank you, child of mine,
Now woman
Full of grace, life,
And the same loving smile

Child I never dreamed
Born from a little girl's wish
A child of bright eyes
But different slightly
And so the generations shift
Seeing life
From another perspective.

**Unarmed**

Thick scales fall
Leaving my skin exposed
To the elements and rushing sounds,
Feelings I'd long since let rust
Upon the rocky surface
Melting into only dust.
How could I let myself
Step outside my armor clad
Shell of safety?
Why walk with mindless abandon
Through this dangerous land
With no protection or reserve?
Am I awake to sense the danger
I have so utterly ignored?
Why must I take this path?
Do I fail to understand
How silly is this giddy venture?
Yet I feel so free, released,
Blind to reason and warnings
As I enjoy
The sweet, succulent satisfaction
Of an afternoon's passing —
One dripping, delicious moment
Splashing past the other
Marking what was
From what will be.

## And What Did You Do with the Gown?

Do you recall the first frigid evening of winter
The wind was seeking to force its way in.
I built a fire and stoked it
Until it snapped at me.
My face was burning with more than heat.
I rose and went to get the gown,
To take it to its end.

I slipped the peachy colored wisps
Inside the grate
Dropping it into the fire.
The heat rolled it gently at first.
The flames began to lick up the airy froth,
Loudly gorging its fierce mouth.
The lovely skirt leaned against the screen
But soon it slid down against the logs
As the delicate lace turned brown and crisp.
A unique and recognized scent floated
Above the smell of charring oak,
While the fire steamed and hissed
Consuming the remaining strands.

The jagged, grabbing arms of the flames
Turned softer
Altering into quieter patterns.

The next morning there was little
To sweep out the hole
With the rest of the ashes.

## Long Gone Memories

There's a bell in the Catholic tower
Shaping the hours with its ringing.
An apartment with blue sky for a background,
For interest — the Texas seacoast over there —
And wild gulls swinging down low for lunch,
With you and me on an apathetic noon,
A day, following days of rain,
With the residents ready to sell the place cheap,
Tomorrow, give it away.
A puzzle of steps under the hill,
To take you from down to up in the town.
Rich men's sailboats lined up,
A free form picket fence,
Keeping the water away.
The car radio with a disc jockey blare —
"CC by the seaside"
So constant you no longer hear,
You, me — suntanned, lazy,
All a haze, quiet and gray —
Repeating sound of the sea.
Long gone memories.

**Delaware Road**

Old barns of stately grace
Stand like dowager queens,
Wearing ancient crowns on weary heads.
They squirm their grey and white,
Aged, patchwork sides into their robes
Of green velvet grass,
Pulling the edges carefully close.
The pond,
The hoarded jewel,
Glitters brilliantly in early morning.
These remaining vestiges of a romantic past
Watch silently out with dark eyes
At the frantic every day —
A quaint, pastoral canvas
Lost beside the freeway
A hectic rush
Of passing cars.

## Midnight Tune

As I travel back the highway,
Ribs of silver seaming
Passing on my right,
To mark the distance back
To my native space,
I am melancholy,
With a body full of love,
Exotic foods, foreign wines.
I wonder,
Why is it that,
With a land full of men,
I must just long for your face?
Why must I hear your voice,
And heed your counsel,
And touch just this one hand?
Why does it matter?
Can I not see
It is certainly like thousands
I passed this day?
But no, I must dream, agonize, ponder
As I listen to a midnight tune
On the radio.
Is this all there is
When you have left once more?
Counting the little markers
That signal the miles away from you?
Knowing that if the backdrop changes
I might never see you again.

**Passing By**

There was a time when I once felt
I could not make it past these hills,
Fencing in my world,
No way out to the other side.
All inside this gentle space,
Where in winter
Stiff, white smoke
Pulls up in frigid skies,
And layered snow comes year on year,
So I could not tell the difference.
I found out it was the trees
That gave the hills their size.
I stumbled through to find freedom's place,
Lived for years on the other side.
I've come back because now I know
I can find my way out.
Still as I walk the ridge before going down,
My hands begin to sweat,
As if it were the height I fear.
Not so
It's the feelings I had left
So far behind.

## The Face in the Jar

Checking my face
in my dressing table mirror,
I am not surprised to view
my fragmented vision.
One hundred tiny fractions,
shattered, puzzle pieces,
collected patterns.
still hinged,
slightly.

I dip my fingers in the cool cream
and smooth it across the cracks
gently pasting
all the parts
into place.

Cool Bitch;
Sweet Wife;
Ugly, Overbearing Mother;
Tyrant, Acid Tongued;
Sexy Sounding
Lover;

Scared, lonely,
lovely woman.
Softly, slowly
hiding,
covering all the lines,
erasing all the signs,

Now I can make up my face.

**Kite Strings**

Your love has set me free
As a child's kite
In
March air,
Bound
Only by the string
Of your tugging presence.
I soar,
Whirl,
Spin
Crazily high
Above the plain
Of ordinary things.
I cannot see the tulips
Pushing through
The winter's reluctant earth.
But the air is magic, rarefied.
I can go great distances safely,
If you do not let me go.

**Long Distance**

Across the twisted network of wires
Out of the dusty depths
Your voice comes to me
Rising to full consciousness
My closeted emotions
Take full flight.
My mind is once more set on edge
To parry with a list of "Should I?"
The coil of the line
Spanning the distance,
Binding for a few brief minutes
All my life to yours,
All my fragile resolutions
Dissolve in anguish.
Don't disconnect! Don't let me go!
The steady buzzing in my head
Resonating,
Repeating,
You are gone again.

## Dream Raker

Dream raker,
Moon bagger,
Star stealer,
On this silver spot
Gather clouds
Beneath our feet
So we may gaze
To worlds beyond,
Collecting dreams
Within our eyes.
Spin
Galaxies
This way,
For our private viewing.
After timeless,
Golden
Hours,
Lifetimes
Multiplied,
We'll fling them
Back
Across the sky.
We will mount
Some rainbow ray
And on a crayon colored beam
We'll touch back
To earth again.

**Separation**

In bright sunshine,
Without you near,
It all seems so clear and easy,
Questions all but disappear.
My loneliness for you
Answers every one.
You should be in my life,
And strife should end.
It seems so simple,
That I could reach out,
Touch you once again.
You would turn to me.
All doubts would be gone.
Then you arrive,
You sit in my presence,
But not close,
You listen and don't hear,
What I would whisper,
If my thoughts could make words?
That I love you.
My rage and frustration
Come so often,
Because you love me
So little,
Want me with you
So seldom,
And need me
Not at all.

**Insight**

The tight, dark circle was drawn up
Like a spring,
Resting coolly within the deep
Pupil of your eye,
Gazing out on lands and fun
That you were searching.
It spiraled outward and I was caught
Upon this coil, as it glinted,
Looking out on me.
Drawn into the center,
Whirled into its inner spaces,
I measured each day
By where that ring rested.
Sucked downward into the joy
Of being held by your voice, dreams, arms,
It seemed as if the orb
Had widened till it held
All life within its sphere.
I careened downward,
Bumping crazily past all the barriers
I had been tethered by.
Then it happened —
the spring was all the way
Out —
So it snapped
Back.

I was outside, as the center
Tightened again
To pinpoint size,
To become, once more,
The pupil of your eye.

**The Visit**

Scorched in hot, vapid spaces
No room to breathe,
Lying here waiting,
Desperate for sleep to come to me,
Your vision returns,
Like some Phoenix,
From ashes long since cold,
You come to visit me.
A long day wildly wasted
Spent tracing the pattern
Of a butterfly's wing,
Counting clouds drifting
Over our heads.
Cupping these delicate images
Within my hands,
I fold the tissues carefully
Over these memories,
To store them again.
Why do you wait
To find your chance
To escape the dark passageways
Of my brain,
Insisting on seeing me,
When I should least see you?

**Eclipse**

My world was solitary, pastoral and plain,
Hardly worth a stranger's glance
As I moved across the land.
A lone figure,
My path a twisted thread,
Vacant but for dirt stirred
By my shuffling feet.
Then as Jupiter aligned with the moon
My world shifted in its orbit.
There you were, between light and earth,
Casting shadows, as if in fog or smoke,
All but your face obscured.
The axis rotated again.
The landscape is burned bare
By the terrestrial firestorms
Of your presence.
My ordinary life is gone.
I am stunned, frozen in place,
But with a peculiar brilliance —
Radiation —
From your nearness.

## Cry for Vietnam

Swish, swish, went the cotton
Over the faded, red color,
"I'm from Ohio — where are you from?"
              "Vietnam"

"Oh, that's so far away. But I'm far away, too.
Ohio is a long way away."
Scratch, scratch, as the file
Shapes to perfectly rounded nails.
"It must be hot like here?"
Heat, bouncing off the brick walls
Lining Dallas' big houses,
Reverberating off miles of concrete.
"I miss the laughter — at holidays."

        Holidays, laughter, silliness,
        Foreign ideas in a foreign land.

"I miss the trees."
Polish slipping down over tiny curves.

        Trees — jungle trees,
        Dense forests — not like any forest here,
        And cries of birds, with different songs.
        "I was a little girl."

"Oh, I guess you don't remember much?"
Whirr, whirr, of the nail dryer starting.

"Come, dry hands!"
        So I won't have to listen
        To the calls of my heart
        And feel the pinch in my soul
        Any longer.

**Peaches**

Let's go to the peach orchard
To spend the afternoon,
Where we'll be all alone,
With the loudest sound,
A buzz of bees.
The sun will beat down between the leaves,
And grass, a zigzag of sunlight and shadow.
Soft dirt will roll into our shoes as we walk.
We'll stroll hand in hand,
Under the umbrella'd trees.
Reaching up I'll pick this one for you.
Check its softness with the press of your fingers
On its bright, blushed, golden skin.
Lift it to your mouth and taste
The sweet, slightly sharp juices
Letting them roll down your throat.
The sticky, lush liquid will be on your chin.
As you consume the fruit,
You follow me with your eyes.
I will also yield to you.
With a little time to ripen in your sun,
No peach could ever match my taste.

## Heartwaves

Tiny rivulets seeping,
Dampening a hidden spot
Long dry,
Now gurgling up,
From a renewed wellspring
Far below.
Pulsing upward through cracks
Wrought by a drought of years,
From an eternity of dust.
The cool slivers streaking,
Dripping, trickling,
Slipping down
The granite face of yesterday,
Past the craggy other side
Growing into streams,
Throbbing into rivers.
Noisily rising,
Rushing,
The sound of waves
Becoming booming breakers —
Heartwaves —
Crashing, pounding, thundering
Against the rocks of silence.

**Dream Capsules**

It's the giving that counts,
Ourselves exposed
To each other's sight.
It's when we're open
That it happens,
Some sweet substance
Flowing
Between us,
Energizing for the time ahead.
Crystallize this world,
This time.
Hold it in some dark,
Hiding place.
If I call,
Send it to me.
When it arrives
I'll blow softly
On the dream.
It will come
To life again.

## Lucy Lee

I could hear in her voice
A different sound,
One of urgency,
A kind of pleading,
But the words the same
As they had always been
"Could you come for a visit?
For just one afternoon?" she'd ask.
"I have a stitch to teach you
I know you'd like to see.
We could have tea and a piece of cake.
You could sit beside my knee."
So many times we'd both planned dates
And yet there never was time
To make a trip so long.
Sitting in the rickety lawn chair
Under the pear tree,
Now I can hear
The sound of the dog's
Padding feet, nails
Clicking on the bricks.
As we go to check the roses
The air conditioner is working,
Whirring,
Draining down into the hungry folds
Of shaded greens.
The roses are so tall
And full of blooms.
It was a good year for roses ...
I drink my tea alone.
I have all you promised
If I came — except you.

**Displaced**

Turning past this building's edge,
In a glance of sunlight
I thought I saw your face —
You!
Hurrying through the crowds,
My feet followed faster,
Lights began to flash.
I ran
Only to lose you in the crush of others.
I searched the yellowed files of my mind
To look up your number
And call
To say,
I thought I saw you yesterday?

**Nightmares**

Come, little sister,
Listen to me.
I cannot sleep this night.
I've had awful dreams
That I must tell you but
I do not know if I was sleeping.
I mounted an elevator
That screamed to the top
And then kept right on going.
It was fifteen stories
Above the clouds
But still kept moving.
I must have been almost to heaven,
When it stopped,
I looked around.
What terrible panic seized me.
Little sister,
Dry my tears, tell me
How will I ever get down?
You know how I hate heights.

## Clock Clicks

Mock eternity sets itself
Within our being,
Casting its repetitions
Inside our souls,
Wearing us down
With the sorrow
Of a thousand years
Upon this earth.
And you seek a new image?
One moment lost,
As the clock flicks off
The Present
Into the vast
Unconscious wastes
Of enfolding air
Time flicks off
Present to Past —
Refrain of my youth
Come back again,
From Life
To Remembrance
To Life,
Relived
Within the sketch
Of Purpose,
Placed within a thimble.
"You seek the Truth
And it shall make you free."
From what?
To what? Ourselves, also?

And the steady
'Plank'
Of rain
Against metal,
Wearing away the world
To a race
Of soft shaved
Rust.

*1960*

## People

Old man on the street corner,
Standing,
Watching
Whose face marks more than years
Tells of all time.
People that stand —

Short woman with shoes that pinch,
Walking,
Listening,
Who treads the nine to ten shift
The long beat.
People that walk —

Child whose mind is all hurry,
Running,
Yelling,
Who must do something
Quickly,
Tomorrow never comes.
People that run —

People that stand —
People that walk —
People that run —
Come
Before the whistle's blown,
Before the flag is downed,
Before the gate is closed
People,
Come

*1959*

**Solo**

All the light is gone.
The sky is darkened,
The candle out.
The room is cold,
The wind is up,
Chilling the corners,
You are gone.
It's not just a matter
Of me not filling up
The hollow spaces of your arms,
But half of me —
An arm, a leg, half a soul —
Out there somewhere,
Wandering around as a man,
Making love to a horn.
All of warmth, peace
Behind some magic door,
Lost in the mist
Of a piper's foggy promises.

**Chance Encounter**

What has brought us to this place,
A chance encounter of old lovers?
Are there words left to say,
Wishes to ponder?
The hustle around us is gone,
All is still and quiet,
As if some knob has been turned.
We are alone in the shoving crowd.
We speak not at all,
Actors who have forgotten every line.
What fantasy could transpire,
Not in our dreams,
But this once waking?
The noise has returned,
Ancient ritual, shaking hands,
Brief greetings.
We pass by
To the other side.

**Night Call**

It's not that I love you less,
Or more,
But differently now.
The passion, always present,
Never changed from before,
But now finding you again,
I feel a sense of caution,
A tempering of time ,
That makes me know —
Seasons change,
We change,
Even love changes.
What has not changed
Is my need for your nearness
So still, in the night,
I begin my vain search for you.
I pause, my finger on the numbers,
Fighting off my surrender.
When does acceptance begin?

## New Year's Day

No one, no one
Hears my voice,
My calm recitation of interior needs.
Like some lost Chilean miner
I call up from my depths,
The echoes rambling upward,
Bouncing from my sides,
But no sound can make it
To the top.

Can you not see
My sorrow so etched
In the mask my face becomes?
So many dreams surrendered,
Given over as ransom
To maintain a daily living.
Each day lies upon the other
Like some tipsy, topsy cake
About to fall.

What is left?
How much time?
Enough to rise like
Some lauded oldster
With tales of triumph?

I am lost to all my desperation.
Spinning in memorized circles,
Going nowhere.
And my life slips closer
To the edge of the end.
 I sit, gnawing at myself,

Knowing, I've never
Ever, ever tried
To abandon what I've been.
Crying silently,
The tears are dripping inside
Leaving me awash, afloat.

Enough of this lamenting.
Too much of the day spent like this!
Time to wash the dishes and the dog
And carry lunch to my mom.

Frothy clouds piling up
The sun might break through.
Each year a new beginning!
With a quick discarding of my resolutions,
They are lost with the leftover confetti on the floor.

Ah, now I can put this day behind me and go on.

## The Vigil

I came in the door and she said you were nearly gone.
Gone? How could you be gone
when I have had you with me all these years?
How could you be gone
when you have not spoken for days?
There is so much for me to say and you to hear.

So many times I did not treat you
with the love I had for you.
I withheld it, angry at your disinterest.
You cared for others and depended on me.
And now you'd just leave?

Leave me to ponder,
to wrestle long days with my conscience,
holding my feelings inside me, unspoken.
You would leave me to suffer
for not saying the words I should have.

I feel an urgency to do something
to stop this natural progression.
How can I keep you?
How can I make you wait?
The tears are all pouring in a torrent
Through my body,
But they are not coming from my eyes.

I gather you up, hold you to me.
Lying there in the heat of dying
your back is still warm.
The bed is damp from perspiration,
while your body is so quickly cooled.

Now the grief is washing over me.
Crying, crying, it's too late,
Tears falling to my waist, my hands.
They flow so fast they never streak my cheeks.
The words come.
They rush out,
for you to know
but you can no longer hear.

Your breathing has stopped now.
One last effort
and you are gone.
I am here and bereft, grieved --
As if I had no idea you would ever go.

**Void**

Sorrow smothers me like a blanket
In the heat of a summer's day
For I know I could not be living
My heart has nothing to say.

## Breaking the Tape in the Nuclear Arms Race

Bruised sky,
Charred land,
Scarred marble
That is Earth.
The sun is clouded,
Moon is gone,
Did anyone know
What went wrong?
There was an accident?
Someone went mad?
The button was hit
All the rest is obscured.
Dust,
Rubble,
Silence long.
The Earth whirls past
While stars collide.
The Ice Age comes again
With monstrous storms
But none were disasters
That were feared.
That is reserved
For those who live.
No one did.

*1961*

**Album**

Blue and gold edge brilliant
Against the charcoal dark
Of Florida's wet night.
The rain has ended
As day rises, bleeding light
And color
Into the landscape.
The quiet sea moves slowly
From its rest,
Waves stretching out
In a lazy yawn.
Everywhere the dew captures
The ordinary,
Sparkling the world,
Like diamonds magnified.
This morning greets us,
Two indolent lovers,
With no agenda,
In time standing still,
Etched in my mind's photograph.

**Conflagration**

Small flame, which grew
Burned the darkness
To make it day
Still consume.
Turn to ashes at my feet
All former barriers —
Leave me gutted and bare
Ready for rebuilding.

**Retrospect**

Yesterday is ten miles back,
Tomorrow a short way forward,
Yet I only long for yesterday
And fear to reach tomorrow.
My mind would ask
For one more day
But my heart
Wants only yesterday.
The sounds of my life
Are the measured gratings
Of my feet upon the walk,
The seagull's cry,
The slipping of water puddles,
As my feet trace
The line of years.

**Reprise**

Finally there you stand
Head raised, face shining,
I see that smile.
My heart longs to answer.
All the days we never knew
The hours, plans, promises,
We never had, nor made, nor gave,
All the 'could have beens',
Hanging as visible strands
Swaying in the space between us.
You stand there,
The light behind you,
In some exquisitely orchestrated
Finale.

The shadows shift.
I have not called you near
In any dark,
And in this jungle grown
Too thick for any man
To casually wander through
You've found this place.
So now you're here,
I am here.
Should we begin again?
Despite my pounding heart,
This time I know —
You are seeing past my eyes.
You are not what
I held you to be.
So am I free?

**Belief**

Rise to sunsinged clouds, unwinged body!
Clasp all earth and passing waters, armless one!
View man and happenings of time, blind form!
Hear natural music and that divine, deaf shape!
Despise all faithless!
Soar,
Embrace,
Witness,
Listen.

**Care Packages**

Our love is bought at a handsome price,
At strange market stalls, exotic fairs,
It must be rationed out
Hoarded like a miser's store.
It must be saved for the lonely needing
Of empty times, empty places,
Spending a little on the frosty dark
Laying away a little to feel 'ok',
When there's too much sun,
Too many people around.
Our love is parceled out,
Care packages from the past.

**Comet**

Pinpoint,
Bright, tiny, faraway,
Shaping, forming, expanding,
Building, growing, casting
A magnificent, beaming light.
Turning, arcing, bending,
Coming, dancing, gleaming,
Flashing, radiating,
Rushing, speeding,
Hurtling, dazzling,
Crowding out the night.
Roaring, exploding,
Fireworks, burning up the sky.
Pulling, passing, going,
Reducing, separating, leaving,
Narrowing, sparklers,
Bright, tiny, faraway
Pinpoints of light.

**Enigma**

This heart knows the secret
Of a full running tide,
Of a plump moon,
Of an Indian summer.
These are the chambers of a heart
Grown bittersweet.

## The Bus Ticket

The large, grey, black windowed bus
Ground to a gravelly stop
Beside the window marked "Café".
The door swung open emitting coolness
From its upholstered cavern
Distilling quickly in the bright, Texas heat.
One lone passenger, a boy of maybe ten or twelve,
Stepped down behind the driver.
The baggage door swung up.
One cardboard box, taped shut,
And a bag with many travel cracks
Were dropped to the broken curb.
The driver bounded back up the steps,
Shutting the door quickly
To keep the coolness in.
The blinkers winking, barely visible in the dust,
The bus turned back to its path.
Crunching the gravel
Into a gritty swirl, it rolled away.
He stood there a moment
As if he had no place to go,
Then picking up his parcel under his arm
He drug his bag along, hitting his leg as he struggled.
Looking first behind him, then ahead
Then behind again,
Stopping beside a telephone post,
To gain its narrow shadow.
He leaned his back for a moment
Against the sticky black post and I
Turned back to my work, wiping the table,
Making wet circles on the pink plastic cloth.
A half hour, then an hour passed.
I looked back out again to see him

Gathering his belongings, he walked up to the window,
Pressing his nose against the glass,
Checking the inside.
The door clicked, the bell rang,
He stood framed against the screen door.
Stuffing his hand down inside the pocket
Of his checkered shirt,
He dropped a few coins and slip of paper
To the scarred and dented, wooden floor.
"Hi," he said, "How much for the orange?"
I looked at his strained face.
Trickles of sweat had traced lines
Across his cheeks, through dust and freckles.
"Twenty-five cents," I answered.
He swung onto the stool,
"How much if I use the phone?"
I wiped my hands on my apron,
"Who you gonna call?"
"Grayson's farm. I have two aunts up there,
Supposed to pick me up. Guess they didn't know
What time I'd come."
"Maybe that's them."
I pointed with my hand that held the rag,
At two old ladies getting out
Of an long, old, white Ford truck
That had pulled onto the lot.
He slipped off the stool, shuffling slowly to the door.
"Don't want that orange," I called.
"Next time, I'll be back," he answered.
That day was the last I saw
The boy in the checkered shirt,
But I saw the story in the paper.

**The Review**

Where did the years go that were given to me?
The childhood spent in fear and a cotton field broiling,
Running always from the home that should have been
A safe and cozy place.

Then a marriage that wasn't military, but corporate,
But you couldn't tell the difference.
I filled a slot, called wife,
Looking for love from babies.
In my hunger, I kept adding to them,
Until the call came,
The universal throwing down of kitchen spoons
And off to somewhere else to work.
Work added to work
And became as hard as cotton rows.

First marriage gone and not grieved at loss,
Second spouse and trouble from the start,
With too many elbows and knees hurting each other
And the whole thing rotting from the inside out.
So it too was gone.

Years of saying goodbye to those babies grown,
Of tears over their own losses of mother's love —
Too empty in the larder and a dad completely missing.
Their own floundering and gasping while trying
To find some way of their own,
In not enough of anything they needed.

Finally some quiet, but too much of it,
So that you wanted to yell stop!
Don't serve me anymore!
I look for those children and they are scattered,
Brimming over with desires and choices,
Their children, with their own knees and elbows,
Poking, sticking.
Longing for a hand in mine.

The last love is now wagered.
It's still harder than I thought it to be
But more desperately sought than those before.
Peace, that quiet respite, settles down.

I sit on the porch and rock and count
The days left
Pondering how to parcel them about.

Looking back it is like when we played cards
As children, shuffling by scattering
And twisting them to mix them up,
So when we dealt them out,
They were still in straights and pairs,
Now the discards, the jokers, the random one,
And in the end the red 3.

## Holy Weak

Palm frond, lying pale green now,
Upon my kitchen counter.
Just the other day I waved you,
Gleeful about the week to come.
Friends, families, chicks and bunnies
So much coming to be enjoyed.

Palm frond, lying greyed, fraying,
These last days my attention waned.
I meant to stay focused but I went to sleep.
Now it is Thursday and the days are trying.
There was the little white lie at the car wash,
Then was I charged for the flowers
At the bottom of the cart?
It was a short retort, not necessary,
To my elderly mother.

Palm frond, lying yellowed and dry,
Rebuking me as I shove it around to cook.
Friday dawns and I can feel what is coming
I will rue my little cherished falsities, my vanity,
And, oh dear, my selfishness — I regret it all.
It won't be enough — the cross will still be raised,
Despite my evasion,
It will still cast its shadow on me.

Palm frond lying withered, wantonly forgotten
This solemn reminder is too morose, so into the trash.
Time to rise for Sunday morning —
Wonderful bright blue sky —
Simmering.

## Taking Out the Seam

For all I do, whatever it is,
You have the answers before
I speak the questions.
However I back away,
I turn to find you there.
You will not leave or let me.
We both know I must
Mold your face back to what it was,
Undo this embroidery of your hand with mine,
Leave you cold and alone
Against what I can't foresee.
It scares me.
I'd like to present you a lifetime supply
Of salve and band aids
And a book of "How to" for eggshell repair.
I love you.
I know you feel that.
May it help you through all
That is and will be.
It stretches out before us
An endless calendar of long afternoons alone.
So please, protect me,
Don't make me exclaim,
"God, what a fall!"

**Morning**

In the corner of my eye
Bright light
Raising me to know
It's morning.
I move each leg slowly in the bed
To see if I'm dreaming
No — a form lies beside me.
I push and move back.
Not awake, but answering,
Your arm moves around my waist.
I snuggle backwards into your hold.
Let me soak up your nearness
Stealing a few moments
Before the spinning day.
I turn the pillow over and now
Its case is cool.
My breath tells me
The room is cold.
I pull back inside my warm shell.
Let's wait two more minutes,
Dreaming and holding out,
Against the sounds that tell
This day begins.

## Ice Palaces

Forgive me for not letting all
The barriers down,
But I would have held you so close.
As I warmed, I would have begun
To weep.
Someday I will write you reams
On Arctic survival,
On how to live in days of ice,
Frozen,
Alone,
In palaces of frigid air.
I'll write you the way to last,
In cold and empty spaces,
In the hollow rooms
Of your mind.

**Place of Rest**

I lie down in grass
Sun on my face,
Becoming partner to earth.
I bloom
Under an unfettered sky.
Shade cools me,
The sun warms me,
Joy fills me
As I hear
The soft lowing of cattle nearby.
I gaze out at sunsets and moon rises,
Sleeping quietly in rain

**Ennui**

My heart is like a turned down cup
Empty and unwilling to be filled
And all the petty things about me
The saucer that it sits upon.

**Bargain**

I was one of the great unlearned
And you?
You were one of the elegant wounded.
In the strange way of destined things
We were joined
As egg yolks to egg whites
Lungs to breath,
Babies and Life.
You to teach
Me to mend.

**After The End**

The singsong monotone of a plane
Telegraphs a drying loneliness

> Do you remember or care or wish
> It could be done over?

Wouldn't it be nice to be so old, uncaring
That a jet's arc in sunlight
Couldn't bring a shingle shiver?

> You'd have to swear not to smile
> Or crinkle your eyes,
> Or laugh.

You were only an ordinary man. It's just the 5:40 from the Southwest.

> We couldn't walk the beach in solitude
> holding hands,
> for that love,
> and the end of it,
> would all come back.

I'm busy living. I made it to the other side.

> I miss you,
> no matter what others hear me say.
> It seems only fair that the world should stop.

**Prospecting**

I take my pen, as pan,
And begin to sift,
Bent to work to shake,
Straining the words, searching
For a word, or phrase.
The pools of the random lot,
Swirling, around and around,
Some splashing out and gone,
Some staying, floating upwards.
As I pore over them,
Through streams of thought,
To glean a nugget,
In hopes a richer vein is struck,
Desiring that kind of gold
That's seldom found.
First the work is slow.
Words trickle and
Sometimes little comes
Or surprisingly they pour fast
In gushers through the cracks,
Past other random thoughts
To maybe glint, perhaps, shine?
Turning each one to see,
I examine what remains,
Not really knowing,
Is it fool's gold
Or miner's find?

## Bio: Patricia Ingle McCarty Castrinos Ruth

Patricia Ingle McCarty Castrinos Ruth was born in Corpus Christi, Texas, attending both Del Mar College in Corpus Christi and Methodist Theological Seminary in Delaware, Ohio.

One of her poems was published in a local tourist magazine when she was 18 years old. She has shown the remainder of her poetry, with few exceptions, to no one outside of her immediate family and the closest of friends. She has written a self-published cookbook, <u>Cooking with My Grandmothers, Old Texas Recipes from 1900-1970</u>, and has recently written two novels.

Patricia Ann Ruth lives in Round Rock, Texas, with her husband, Jim. She is the mother to four, stepmom to one, and enjoys 16 splendid grandchildren. All four of the daughters are writers and one is a noted artist. Her son is an encryption and streaming video guru. She and her husband enjoy golf, gardening, doing volunteer work, travel and spending time with their family.

# INDEX

40 Knots .................................................. 34
A New Orleans Goodbye ......... 116
A Soldier's Peace ........................ 172
A Tie That Binds ........................ 160
Accounting .................................. 40
After The Blake Exam ................. 63
After The End ............................ 281
Ah, Eve ........................................ 29
Ah, Tchaikovsky! ....................... 169
Album ....................................... 262
Anacahuita .................................. 13
And What Did You Do with the
  Gown? ................................... 230
At A Grave .................................. 55
Backward Slider .......................... 10
Bargain ...................................... 280
Barren ......................................... 67
Before the morning rises ........... 127
Belief ......................................... 266
Bio: Faith Patricia Williams Ingle
  Collins ..................................... 86
Bio: Laura P. McCarty ............... 131
Bio: Patricia Ingle McCarty
  Castrinos Ruth ...................... 283
Bio: Penny Faith Ingle Bagby ... 205
Blessed Curse ............................ 124
Breaking the Tape in the Nuclear
  Arms Race ............................ 261
Brief Sensations ......................... 108
Brief Sojourn ............................. 202
Care Packages ........................... 267
Chalk Story ............................... 163
Chance Encounter ..................... 254
Child of Mine ............................. 83
Cleo's Snake .............................. 218
Clock Clicks .............................. 250
Comet ........................................ 268
Confessional ................................. 7
Conflagration ............................ 263
Conflict! .................................... 171
Confrontation ............................. 74
Cottontails ................................ 148
Creating .................................... 204

Cry for Vietnam ......................... 243
Daughter Mine .......................... 228
Death in Mexico ......................... 22
Death Was Different Then ........ 138
Delaware Road .......................... 232
Deprivation ................................. 70
Dialogue ..................................... 44
Discards ...................................... 50
Disconnect .................................. 54
Displaced .................................. 248
Dispossessed ............................ 164
Dream Capsules ........................ 246
Dream Raker ............................. 238
Drought .................................... 224
Durable Foe ................................ 58
East Texas Morning .................... 28
Eclipse ...................................... 242
Eden's Exile ................................ 35
Endowment .............................. 159
Enigma ..................................... 269
Ennui ........................................ 279
Escape Plan .............................. 154
Esperanza ................................. 183
Et je rapelle ................................ 76
Exposed .................................... 186
Ezekiel ....................................... 31
Façade ........................................ 43
Facsimile .................................. 162
Family Anthology ..................... 201
Far Sojourner ............................ 215
Feather in the Wind ................. 145
Flight To Zion ............................. 37
Fly By Love .............................. 117
F o g ......................................... 155
For Crying Out Loud .................. 42
Forest Oasis ............................. 209
Forgiving Child ........................ 167
Grabbing the Ring .................... 225
Heartwaves ............................... 245
Holy Weak ................................ 274
Hosea's Wife .............................. 30
I dislocated my heart to silence the
  belly of my soul ...................... 94

285

| | |
|---|---|
| I don't think swings were made for women's hips | 126 |
| Ice Palaces | 277 |
| Illusion | 26 |
| Image | 165 |
| Impasse | 47 |
| Impotence | 41 |
| Inland Alien | 24 |
| Insight | 240 |
| Insolent Insomnia | 146 |
| Interview with Discovery | 192 |
| Jackrabbits | 144 |
| Journey | 99 |
| July in Houston | 79 |
| June of '67 | 81 |
| Kaleidoscope | 180 |
| Kite Strings | 236 |
| Lament | 199 |
| Lament from a Fig Tree | 217 |
| Le Professeur | 64 |
| Legacy | 11 |
| Life's Bookkeeping | 226 |
| Listening to Kuwait | 109 |
| Lonely Places | 49 |
| Long Distance | 237 |
| Long Distance Camera | 20 |
| Long Gone Memories | 231 |
| Loren Eiseley | 75 |
| Lot's Wife | 36 |
| Lucifer or Lochinvar! | 27 |
| Lucy Lee | 247 |
| Lunar Ritual | 196 |
| Map of the World | 91 |
| Margarita with Salt | 152 |
| May-Istrom | 150 |
| Mea Culpa | 25 |
| Meet Me Beneath the Sitka Spruce | 111 |
| Merry-Go-Round | 5 |
| Midnight Tune | 233 |
| Mirage | 214 |
| Mirror | 82 |
| Mood Music | 182 |
| Moonflood | 19 |
| Morning | 276 |
| Morning Surprise | 120 |
| Moving On | 221 |
| Mowing In Summer | 80 |
| New Beginnings — A Villanelle | 178 |
| New Orleans Goodbye | 116 |
| New Year's Day | 256 |
| Night Call | 255 |
| Nightfall | 53 |
| Nightmares | 249 |
| Nolle Prosequi | 33 |
| Number Twenty-One | 65 |
| Oaken | 187 |
| Observatory Place | 100 |
| Odyssey | 8 |
| Of Saints and Sinners, Mostly Sinners | 60 |
| On Making Poetry | 85 |
| On Weeping | 16 |
| Painted Woman/Painted Fathers | 107 |
| Palette | 181 |
| Passage | 48 |
| Passing By | 234 |
| Pavane | 21 |
| Peach Colored Pills | 113 |
| Peaches | 244 |
| People | 252 |
| Persistence | 151 |
| Personalities in Wood | 179 |
| Petition — A Villanelle | 168 |
| Piece of Glass | 140 |
| Place of Rest | 278 |
| Porter for My Dreams | 222 |
| Prayer | 17 |
| Prayer at Seventeen | 227 |
| Prospecting | 282 |
| Radiology | 118 |
| Rain | 77 |
| Recess in Tynan | 158 |
| Reckoning | 52 |
| Reoccurring | 112 |
| Reprise | 265 |
| Requiem for Discovery | 189 |
| Residue | 185 |

| | |
|---|---|
| Respite ............................................ 23 | The Enlightened ............................. 9 |
| Retrospect ..................................... 264 | The Face in the Jar ..................... 235 |
| Re-vision ...................................... 137 | The Fig Thief ................................ 114 |
| riddle ............................................... 73 | The Friend .................................... 143 |
| Roses ............................................... 57 | The Happy Boys .......................... 66 |
| Saturday Chores ........................ 106 | The Placid Warrior .................... 98 |
| Second Verse .............................. 156 | The Praying of the Creed .......... 173 |
| Selection ........................................ 12 | The Primitive ................................ 3 |
| Sentimental Journey .................. 136 | The Question — A Villanelle .... 142 |
| Separation ................................... 239 | The Review .................................. 272 |
| Serpentes Doggeralis .................. 14 | The Slow One .............................. 72 |
| Shhh .............................................. 149 | The Tally ....................................... 61 |
| Showtime ..................................... 220 | The Unburdened ......................... 51 |
| Sic Transit ..................................... 32 | The Valley Boy's Homecoming .. 62 |
| Silent Witnesses ........................... 68 | The Vigil ....................................... 258 |
| Solitary Night-Shift Man ............. 71 | The Visit ....................................... 241 |
| Solo ............................................... 253 | The Wedding Jewels .................. 184 |
| Sometimes ................................... 122 | The Weight of You .................... 103 |
| Song of a Kentucky Visit ........... 210 | To Maya ....................................... 104 |
| Spring Cleaning .......................... 190 | To My Mother (Mother's Day, 1979) ......................................... 166 |
| Spring Organum .......................... 18 | Transplanted .............................. 188 |
| Spring Rain ................................... 78 | Turning Aside ............................. 216 |
| Stones from the Jordan ............... 46 | Turning the Dirt .......................... 96 |
| Story on the Rim ........................ 105 | Unarmed ...................................... 229 |
| Summation .................................... 45 | Vanity of Vanities ...................... 195 |
| Sweeping Up Shards ................. 200 | Vernal Exhibitionists ................. 194 |
| Taking Out The Seam ............... 275 | Victory Sonnet ............................. 84 |
| Texas Tunes ................................ 110 | Viens à moi ................................. 125 |
| The Benediction ......................... 128 | Void .............................................. 260 |
| The Box .......................................... 38 | VOWS ............................................ 39 |
| The Bus Ticket ............................ 270 | When August turns to October 130 |
| The Butter Knows ...................... 157 | White Beauty .............................. 170 |
| The Caretaker ............................... 92 | Who Art In Heaven ..................... 4 |
| The Challenge ............................... 59 | With Strings Tied ......................... 6 |
| The Day in the Navy Dress ...... 212 | Wordsworth — USA, 1992 ....... 135 |
| The Delivery ................................. 56 | Writing Poetry ............................ 203 |
| The Doves ................................... 198 | |
| The Drought ............................... 153 | |

www.ingramcontent.com/pod-product-compliance
Lightning Source LLC
Chambersburg PA
CBHW030635150426
42811CB00077B/2106/J